WANDI

&

WONDERING

(Lent in the Byways of the Bible)

with
DAVID DUNN-WILSON

All profits from the sale of this book will be channelled
through the Cliff College International Training Centre
(CCITC) Account and used for the support of the
families in Uganda of ministers who are being trained
in the Kenya Methodist University (KeMU). Other
donations welcomed!

A CIP catalogue record for this title is available from
the British Library.

Thanks to Mr Barry Myers for Book Cover pictures:
Front Cover: Sunset, Crow Park, Keswick
Back Cover: Ynys Llanddwyn (Llanddwyn Island),
Newborough, Anglesey

To my spiritual family,

The Methodists

of

Gamelands and Cross-in-Hand

FOREWORD

In the Christian calendar, Lent is a special time. The run-up to Easter is enriched by Christians reflecting on Jesus spending forty days and nights alone in the wilderness. It is a great time to work out deep things in our life. We can look at our attitude to others. We can reflect on the wonder of the Cross and ask God's forgiveness for mistakes we have made. It is certainly a time to deepen our Christian discipleship.

During Lent, Christians often have some kind of discipline to aid them. I always have a 'Lent book' and I earnestly commend this one to you. It is written with such remarkable honesty and skill that our own Lenten meditations cannot fail to be sparked and deepened as we are led through some of the Bible's less familiar passages.

It is an honour for me to write the Foreword to this book. Professor David Dunn-Wilson is a man I deeply respect and hold in high regard. He has often helped me in my walk with Christ and, although he is a man of tremendous learning and academic depth, he has the gift of making ideas clear and helping people. His family pedigree in the Methodist Church goes back to the time of John Wesley and his children and grandchildren continue to serve the Church in faith today. He is an evangelist at heart with a passion to draw people closer to Jesus. Read and enjoy this book. Meditate upon it and be blessed in your Lenten reading

STEVE WILD (Revd.)
President of the Methodist Conference (2015-2016)

AN INVITATION:

The Bible is a map of Grace which gives access to a network of roads leading us to God. It has its splendid Motorways – the 'fast-track' highways along which we speed to precious truths (*Psalms, the Gospels* and the great *Epistles* spring to mind). It also has its 'A Roads' – those well-tried major routes leading to precious guidance and inspiration.

But what about it's 'B Roads' – those by-ways not so often explored? Indeed, some roads are so rarely travelled that grass grows unmolested on their tarmac. Announce a reading from one of these books in Sunday worship and even seasoned worshippers surreptitiously have to consult their Bible's Index.

Yet these books are part of God's Word. God has put them on the map for a purpose and I ought not to ignore them. Wondering how God might use them to speak to me, I have decided to wander through them for my Lenten devotions. Whatever I discover, I will write down, so that again, as last year for some of you, you can look over my shoulder and read my mind.

Some of the paths may be so neglected that I will need to remind myself why they are there and where they lead. However, this is not a scholarly commentary. I think of it more as a sort of *Wainwright's Walks* which, instead of taking me through Lakeland glories, records my pilgrimage along the Bible's by-ways. Most of my chosen 'B Road' books are short and may easily be read in their entirety, but, from them, I will select verses that have made me pause and think more carefully.

For me, and I trust for many of you, It will be like taking a country walk when some striking view stops me in my tracks and compels me to look and learn a little more.

Please use my thoughts as your starting-point but do not stop there. I am a very imperfect Christian and your spiritual eyes may well be sharper than mine. Using your spiritual varifocals, you will see flowers in the hedgerows that I have missed and discern distant vistas hidden by my spiritual myopia. That is the way God's Word works. It alerts our spiritual senses so that we receive personal revelations. Why not carry a note-book with you and jot down your private thoughts and visions as you walk?

So I invite you to put on your walking-boots. Let us set out together on a pilgrimage into Lent and see where God will lead us.

David Dunn-Wilson
November 2016

N.B. *For quotations, except where another version is indicated I have used the Contemporary English Version of the Bible because it seems to me to capture the mood of the Scriptures so vividly but, by all means, compare it with other versions to gain additional insights. I have chosen Key Verses for each day, but there is also plenty of 'food for thought' in the remainder of the passages chosen for reading.*

TABLE OF CONTENTS

ECCLESIASTES

1: "A BRIDGE TOO FAR"

Reading: Eccl. Chapter One   **(Key: Verse 2)**

"Nothing makes sense. Everything is nonsense"

I have heard it so often in sermons – the story of the lost traveller who, when asking directions from a country bumpkin, is told, "If I were you, sir, I wouldn't start from here." It doesn't make me laugh any more, but it has suddenly become very appropriate. My prescient wife has just said, "For heaven's sake don't start with *Ecclesiastes* or nobody will want to read any further." But it's too late. I have already started and I can only hope that, just for once, her unfailing omniscience has had an 'off day'.

However, I understand what she means. Reading this book seems to lead to 'Futilityville' – the town whose coat of arms bears the motto, "All is Vanity!" I see that the book's original title is *Qoheleth* – an official who calls meetings, 'a preacher' or 'teacher' – but what the book is all about is a puzzle

Some experts say that the author is talking to himself – a sort of ancient *Hitchhiker's Guide to the Galaxy,* whose writer is searching for, 'the meaning of life, the universe and everything'. Other experts think that it is just a scholarly debate, the record of an academic seminar. But I like the suggestion that Qoheleth is being ironical. He is quoting materialists' arguments back at them and making them confess what a bleak picture they paint. If those experts are right and the book is a challenge to a secular society, what could be more relevant today?

More than thirty times, the Preacher bemoans the fact that things are 'vain'. The original word is linked with 'breath', so it's like saying, "It's just a lot of hot air".

Often I agree with him but I have to draw the line when he says that EVERYTHING is vanity or, as the CEV puts it, "NOTHING makes sense! EVERYTHING is nonsense." Living the whole of life on the assumption that it has neither purpose nor destination drains every experience of meaning and value. That is going too far! Just because *some* things are wrong it does not mean that *everything* is wrong.

But I have to confess that there is one area of life where I can fall into the trap of thinking that way. I easily find myself applying this false principle to people. Just because we 'get off on the wrong foot' or because they have done or said something wrong, I let it colour my whole opinion of them. Of course, deep down I know that it is stupid but I can't seem to help it.

Ridiculously, I expect people to be 'neat'. I expect them to be either wise or foolish, sinners or saints, bad or good, hateful or likeable. What is more, I almost resent it when the fool speaks wisely; or the sinner does saintly things; bad people are generous and hateful people display disarming qualities. Whenever they act out of character it challenges the principle that one moment of 'vanity' means that 'All is vanity'.

I know that Jesus never looked at people that way. Just because Peter sometimes said stupid things, Jesus didn't dismiss him as irredeemably stupid.

In fact, Jesus said that some of Peter's insights came directly from God. Now, that is the sort of attitude I covet. I want to see people as Jesus sees them. I don't want to 'pigeonhole' them or come to them with preconceived ideas. I want to see the best in them and be delighted if I have to revise my bad opinion of them. After all, I need them as much as they need me.

Help us to help each other, Lord,
Each other's cross to bear,
Let each his friendly aid afford
And feel his brother's care.
Help us to build each other up.
Our little stock improve,
Increase our faith, confirm our hope,
And perfect us in love.

Charles Wesley (1707-88)

TODAY'S RESOLVE
I will try my hardest to approach everybody I meet without prejudging them. I will be ready and eager to learn from each encounter.

PRAYER
Lord Jesus, help me to see everybody through your eyes today, especially those that I find it hard to like. Let me see you in everyone. Amen

11

2: "ROUND AND ROUND IN CIRCLES"

Reading: Eccl 1: 9-11   **(Key: Verse 9)**

"Nothing is new, nothing under the sun."

I know what he means. In the news I hear the terrible things that people do and I say to myself, "Here we go again! Will people never learn?" Sometimes the Preacher's idea seems to make sense. Perhaps history is, indeed, a wheel on which the same events are carried around again and again. Perhaps he is right. Is there really any point in trying to change things when "Everything that happens has happened before"?

However, I simply cannot live with that sort of 'dead end' attitude to life. Just out of curiosity, I have looked up the word 'new' in my battered old *Cruden's Bible Concordance* and find that it occurs over a hundred times. I know that the 'numbers game' is a tricky thing, but at least it shows me that, as a Christian, I need to take the notion of 'newness' seriously. If there is 'nothing new under the sun' why does the Bible speak so often of God doing 'new' things - making a 'new covenant', bestowing a 'new spirit', making 'a new creation' and why are Christians, Christ's 'new creatures'?

This apparent clash of ideas has set me thinking. I cling to those lovely words from *The Book of Lamentations* (of all places!). "The mercies of the Lord are new every morning." (3:23) What a wonderful idea!

Every day is not a dull repetition of the day before; it is a new gift of Grace. It is a unique blessing. There has never been a day like it *before* and there will never be a day like it again.

Perhaps that is partly why, for thirty years, I have kept my daily *Journal*. In which I record even trivial events. Every one of those events – even those which are repeated as part of my daily routine - is unique. The *CEV* paraphrases v.8 as, "All life is more boring than words can say" and so it is for many people but it must never be so for me because each day is filled with divine 'newness'. Old John Keble had it right when he wrote,

New mercies each returning day
Hover around us while we pray;
New perils past, new sins forgiven,
New thoughts of God, new hopes of heaven.
If on our daily course our mind
Be set to hallow all we find,
New treasures still of countless price
God will provide for sacrifice.

John Keble (1792-1868)

TODAY'S RESOLVE
I will thank God for his gift of this new day and make a conscious effort to see him at work in all that it contains.

PRAYER
Dear Lord, who touches my life with newness; help me to respond with gratitude and to use this day for your glory. Amen

3: "IGNORANCE IS BLISS"

Reading: Eccl 1:12-18   **(Key: Verse 18)**

"The more you know the more you hurt; the more you understand the more you suffer."

What a strange thing to say! Here is Solomon, the cleverest man in the world; the Super Mastermind who has seen everything and knows everything, saying that it is all 'chasing the wind'. "The less you know the better", he says, "because learning just makes you feel worse". So ignorance is bliss after all.

I don't really know what to make of it, but I have to admit that there are ways in which too much knowledge can be painful.

I realise that, whenever I see television coverage of the most recent tragedy or atrocity. In the past, I would have known nothing about those dreadful happenings but now they enter my heart through eyes that see so much that is tragic. I cannot say, "I didn't know" – and it hurts! More knowledge can certainly bring more disquiet.

I have just thought of another way in which too much knowledge can be a problem. I remember the important lesson I learned from an old saint in the vestry of a Black Country Chapel to which I had been sent as a student preacher. "Remember, young man," he said solemnly, "we don't want none of your theology here. Just give us the simple Gospel."

Obviously he had suffered from student preachers' eagerness to regurgitate their most recent Apologetics lectures! But what was he saying? He was reminding me that not all knowledge is of equal importance. Too many random facts can obscure essential truths just as rampant weeds can choke lovely flowers. So there are ways in which Solomon is right.

But there's something even more disturbing here. If, as I believe, Solomon is challenging people who mindlessly idolize knowledge for its own sake, how this applies to our own society!

Popular opinion assures me that I have an absolute 'right to know' everything about everybody. I am urged to scoop up knowledge, any knowledge, like a rampant JCB – pornography, scandal, gossip, hatred – they all go in!

Rubbish dumps are unhealthy places and any society which mindlessly craves such knowledge soon brings suffering on itself. It loses *Innocence* with its attendant qualities-respect, privacy and trust which unite a healthy society. O dear! I am beginning to sound like a disenchanted old misery but I still think that there is uncomfortable truth here.

I must keep my mind away from the rubbish dump and remember Paul's advice to the Philippians (4:8)

"keep your minds on whatever is true, pure, right, holy, friendly and proper. Never stop thinking about what is truly worthwhile and worthy of praise."

Eternal Light! Eternal Light!
How pure the soul must be,
When placed within Thy searching sight,
It shrinks not, but with calm delight
Can live, and look on Thee!

Thomas Binney (1798-1874)

TODAY'S RESOLVE

Today I will deliberately refuse to give 'house room' to unworthy information.

PRAYER

Lord Jesus, be the censor of my mind and help me to concentrate on good ideas and valuable knowledge. Amen

4: "MY FIFTEEN MINUTES"

Reading: Eccl 2:4-11   **(Key: Verse 11)**

"I thought about everything I had done... and it was simply chasing the wind."

It's over forty years since Andy Warhol predicted that, "in the future everyone will be world famous for 15 minutes" but it still inspires dazzling dreams and endless lines of would-be pop-stars and quiz contestants queuing up for their moment of glory on television.

Yet here is Solomon – the Celebrity of Celebrities. The richest, most famous man in his world; the man who has achieved everything; the man across whose chest, "Been there, done that, got the T-shirt" is emblazoned in diamonds, yet, in the end, he dismisses all of it as 'simply chasing the wind", and declares that "Nothing on earth is worth the trouble." What am I to make of it?

I suppose that, like most people, I want to feel that I have left at least a faint footprint on the sands of time. I don't like the idea of being totally forgotten. It is a human requirement.

I remember how American troops commemorated their presence in wartime Britain by graffiti of a bald-headed man with a prominent nose looking over a wall and saying, 'Kilroy was here'.

More seriously, First World War conscientious objectors, when treated atrociously, defiantly refused to be forgotten. They scratched their names and dates on the walls of their squalid cells in Richmond Castle. The government might have wanted to hide them out of sight but they were determined to show that they had been there.

What is so wrong about wanting to be remembered? Why does Solomon tell me that it is so pointless? The clue lies in his own words, "I got whatever I wanted and did whatever made me happy" and the pronoun 'I' occurs a dozen times in almost as many lines. Solomon is warning me that a life aimed solely at my personal aggrandizement will, indeed, end in 'vanity'.

I think of nihilist pop-groups once famous, now totally forgotten. I think of famous dictators dying in distress, hated in their devastated countries. I think of discredited tele-evangelists, corrupt politicians, and ruthless businessmen all now 'vain' and disgraced. Shakespeare was right,

> *The sceptre, learning, physic must*
> *All follow this and come to dust.*

So is there a right way to be remembered? Some words have just come into my mind (KJV of course!) Paul begins his *Letter to the Philippians,* "I thank my God upon every remembrance of you." Is there, then, a distinctively *Christian* way of being remembered?

Paul says that the reason he remembers the Philippians is "because you have taken part with me in spreading the good news." (v5 CEV) That text sorts me out! All I want to be remembered for is that I 'spread the good news' of Jesus by the things I did and said.

Sadly, much of my life has now passed and my days have been littered with lost opportunities, feeble witnessing and cowardly evasions. But God has given me some 'bonus days' and I can but try to use them properly.

Perhaps, then, I can still say, like the Penitent Thief, "Lord, remember me when you come into your kingdom" and God will smile - and that will be fame enough.

O God, what offering shall I give
To Thee, the Lord of earth and skies?
My spirit, soul and flesh receive
A holy, living sacrifice:
Small as it is, 'tis all my store;
More shouldst Thou have, if I had more.

Joachim Lange (1670-1744) Trans. by John Wesley.

TODAY'S RESOLVE
Today I will do or say something for Jesus that is worth remembering

PRAYER
Lord Jesus, give me an opportunity to witness for you today. When it comes, help me to recognize it and use it. Amen

19

5: "THE LAST SICK JOKE?"

Reading: Eccl 2:12-26　　　　　**(Key: Verse 17)**

"this made me hate life...it's just as senseless as chasing the wind."

I don't feel that I want to linger over this part of *Ecclesiastes*. It is so utterly depressing, but perhaps there are lessons for me even in dark places. It is as though The Preacher is putting all his 'vain' things into a box marked 'Foolishness' and throwing it into the sea.

Now he opens another box, labelled 'Wisdom' believing that, perhaps, that will provide a better clue to living. Scholars argue about the technical definition of 'Wisdom' but, if I'm right in thinking that it means 'understanding how to live life as God intends', this looks very much more promising.

Solomon says that, since he is 'the wisest person who has ever lived in Jerusalem' (1:16), he hopes that he has found the secret of great living. "At least", he says, "the 'wise' are better than the 'fools'". Then, suddenly, his hope pops like a balloon pricked by a pin. He despairs, bewailing the fact that, "Wise or foolish we all die and are soon forgotten" and those who come after us will probably make a mess of all we have tried to do.

Then he just seems to give up the struggle altogether and says, "We might as well enjoy ourselves while we can and just leave God to get on with it."

I was right to be wary of this passage. Whatever lesson can I learn from it? I still cling to the hope that Solomon is being ironical, parodying the view that says, "Death is life's last sick joke which mocks all we try to do."

At my time of life, I'm naturally curious about life after death. I am content to be a godly agnostic about the harmonies of Heaven and the temperatures of Hell. I know little about the furniture of the Great Unknown but of one thing I'm sure - my Lord has never failed me in this life and will not desert me in the next.

However, just supposing that Death were only the 'Gateway to Oblivion', it still would not negate the value of my life. As I see it, Death makes my life more significant not less so. Even my little life leaves marks on the lives of those who know me. Human life is like a relay-race in which, for good or ill, each runner passes the baton to his or her children and friends.

I think of the late Francis Nabieu's fine tribute to my friends Richard and Carole Jackson who were long-term mission partners in Sierra Leone where Francis was President of the Methodist Church. Over twenty years after they had returned to England, he was still insisting that they had never really left Sierra Leone because their work was being continued by the people they had influenced.

I wonder what I will leave behind? I love Shakespeare's picture of Henry V encouraging his weary troops before the battle of Agincourt. He is so effective,

That every wretch, pining and pale before,
Beholding him, plucks comfort from his looks....
......as may unworthiness define,
A little touch of Harry in the night

If my life can only leave 'a little touch of Jesus' in the lives of the people I meet, then 'my living will not be in vain' and I can leave my death in his gentle hands.

Behold the servant of the Lord!
I wait Thy guiding eye to feel,
To hear and keep Thy every word,
To prove and do Thy perfect will,
Joyful from my own works to cease,
Glad to fulfil all righteousness.
Here then to Thee Thy own I leave;
Mould as Thou wilt Thy passive clay;
But let me all Thy stamp receive,
But let me all Thy words obey,
Serve with a single heart and eye,
And to Thy glory live and die.
Charles Wesley (1707-88)

TODAY'S RESOLVE
Today I will try to 'be Jesus' and touch another's life lovingly by what I say or do

PRAYER
Loving Heavenly Father, this day lead me to someone who needs 'a little touch of Jesus' and I am content to leave my last day in your hands. Amen

6: "TURN, TURN, TURN"

Reading: Eccl 3:1-15   **(Key: Verse 1)**

"Everything on earth has its own time and its own season."

I imagine that it must have been the Byrds' recording that made Pete Seeger's 1950s song so famous. *'Turn, Turn, Turn'* transformed this chapter into a pop-song, although few who sang it knew the source of its words. However, I find this passage a strange mixture. There seem to be many ways of understanding it.

For instance, am I to see it as primarily a pessimistic hymn to fatalism? Is the Preacher singing, "God has already got everything sewn up and you can't do anything about it so just make the best of it?" The trouble with this interpretation is that it makes my freewill nothing more than a divine confidence trick. It has been one of history's great theological debates but, whatever the answer, I still cannot believe that a God who shows himself to me in Jesus would play such cynical games. God would not make me think that I am free when really I am a prisoner.

On the other hand, perhaps the Preacher intends me to consider the claim that Pleasure is the main purpose of life. - A sort of 'eat, drink and be merry' song. If God has taken responsibility for everything that happens and nothing I do makes any difference, I am free to indulge myself. (vv. 12-13)

23

I am reminded of Peggy Lee's song with verses tracing a human life with the refrain, "*Is That All There Is?*"

Is that all there is? Is that all there is?
If that's all there is, my friends,
Then let's keep dancing,
Let's break out the booze and have a ball,
If that's all there is.

If nothing that I achieve makes any difference, what is the point of 'doing any work'? Indeed, what is the purpose of my whole life if I cannot make the world a better place than I found it? What is the point of becoming a disciple of Jesus if might just as well be a devotee of Satan?

No, that will not do! I think that, maybe, there is a third option which I find more satisfying. Perhaps the passage is a positive assertion that my life is not unplanned chaos because God has his own timetable for me.

I look back and remember the difficulty of producing the teaching timetable for a university department. There were so many possible variations to consider before the final draft appeared! We knew that it was not the only possible timetable but it was the best one for that situation. What if God's timetable for my life is like that? There are many possible variations on offer but the one he has made is best for me. Accepting that, "Everything on earth has its own time" in a positive way, breathes order into chaos.

However, now for the truly tricky part! I love Bach's cantata "God's time is the very best". If that is true, and God has a 'right time' for events in my life, how do I know when it has arrived? Looking back over my life, I realise that *impatience* has been one of my cardinal sins. Whenever I have tried to hurry God, things have failed because I have not had the patience to wait for the 'inner witness' - that mysterious God-given certainty that the right moment has come.

This passage is, indeed, a patchwork quilt of meanings but this is the one I choose to take. God has not finished with me yet and, when he gives me something new to do, he will assign me the right time to do it.

I will remember that "God's time is the very best time",

Me, if Thy grace vouchsafe to use,
Meanest of all Thy creatures me:
The deed, the time, the manner choose,
Let all my work in Thee be wrought
By Thee to full perfection brought

Charles Wesley (1707-88)

TODAY'S RESOLVE

I will look for God's timetable for today and do what he wants me to do when he wants me to do it.

PRAYER

Loving Lord, I want to do your will in your time. Make me sensitive to the 'inner witness' so that I can be useful for you just where and when you wish. Amen.

7: "WHAT A FRIEND!"

Reading: Eccl 4:9-12   **(Key: Verse 9)**

"You are better off to have a friend than to be all alone."

It was good to struggle with those ideas yesterday even if they did become a little more complicated than I had anticipated but I'm glad to find that today's theme is simpler. The Preacher looks around the world and everywhere he sees injustice and cruelty –a real dose of pessimism. There is only one ray of hope. He says, "If you have to live in such a beastly world, you will cope much better if you face it with a friend." So, today, I can think about the warming subject of friendship.

The anthropologist Robin Dunbar's fascinating study of friendship has taught me to see it as a series of concentric circles. He says that, among my more general acquaintances, I can have an outer circle of about fifty good friends but my inner circle is comprised of about fifteen special friends.

The Preacher becomes quite enthusiastic about the idea because he says that friends give me the joy and support, especially when I am 'feeling down'. Unlike the Preacher, I may not want to sleep with them! In many cultures, beds are not 'private space'. My bed in Sierra Leone on one visit to that country was designed for at least four adults! Nevertheless, friends do warm me when life's chill winds blow and they come to my aid if ever I am under attack.

But I remember that, according to Dunbar, there is one more circle of friendship – the innermost of all. He says that, in that circle, I may have just five 'close friends' – those who are such a part of me that they are truly 'soul mates' and are especially precious.

It interests me that, according to the Old Testament, God seems to have had only *two* such 'close friends' – Abraham and Moses. (II Chron. 20:7, Is. 41:8, Ex.33:11) The idea of belonging to God's innermost friendship circle was so mind-boggling that only two patriarchs were counted worthy of that privilege.

But now something else occurs to me. I hear my Master's voice saying to his disciples, "I speak to you as my *friends* and I have told you everything that my Father has told me." (John 15:15) Is he really telling me that admittance to the inner circle of God's 'close friends' is no longer reserved for solitary patriarchs? Is Jesus saying that divine friendship is open to all who follow him? Is it really open to me so that all the blessings of intimate friendship are mine in Him? What tremendous news!

Watching the faces of a singing congregation is instructive. Some hymns they will sing reluctantly and others dutifully. However, announce, "What a friend we have in Jesus", and they will relax, smile and sing it from the heart. I understand that Joseph Scrivener wrote it in Canada to comfort his lonely mother back in Ireland. But its message is so universal that it retains its hold upon us and it has been translated into many languages.

It touches those every day, peace-threatening situations which make us cry out, like Albert Camus, "Just walk beside me and be my friend"

But how do I activate the blessings of the divine friendship? The hymn gives me the answer with simple directness, "Take it to the Lord in Prayer". Prayer is the conduit through which the Holy Spirit brings me the blessings. Close friends, friends of the innermost circle, do not keep secrets from one another and, if Jesus gives me that privilege, I can hide nothing from him. I can come to him and 'tell it as it is' without any hint of censorship. After his 'Calvary' experience, Jesus is un-shockable. "What a friend I have in Jesus!"

What a Friend we have in Jesus,
All our sins and griefs to bear!
What a privilege to carry
Everything to God in prayer:
O what peace we often forfeit,
O what needless pain we bear,
All because we do not carry
Everything to God in prayer!

Joseph Medicott Scriven (1820-86)

TODAY'S RESOLVE
Today I will read that hymn carefully and think about the words. So often the joy of the music has made me forget the depth of the words' meaning.

PRAYER
Lord Jesus, my Ultimate Best Friend, I thank you for the privilege you have given me. Just walk beside me and be my friend. Amen

8. "SWIMMING IN THE DEEP END"

Reading: Eccl 5:1-7   **(Key: Verses 2 & 7)**

"don't make promises to God without thinking them through ... respect and obey God!"

The Preacher is urging me to be careful when I go to church and not to be like 'the fool' who "makes promises to God without thinking them through." Oddly for me, this warning applies more to hymn-singing than to speaking. I have to confess that I blithely sing hymns which claim profound spiritual experiences that I do not have and I make promises to God that I cannot keep.

For instance, I think of Charles Wesley's glorious hymn, "My heart is full of Christ and longs its glorious matter to declare". In no way can I claim that as an accurate description of my spiritual condition, much as I wish it were. I feel that it's like wearing a T-shirt which claims that I have visited China when I have never even visited Chelsea! Is this 'improper worship'? Ought I to stop singing? But I love singing hymns.

I remember that there was a time when John Wesley had similar misgivings about preaching. He told his friend Peter Bohler that he felt that he must stop preaching because it was hypocritical of him to urge his hearers to have a depth of faith which he himself did not possess. His friend responded, "Preach faith till you have it and then, because you have it, you will preach faith."

By proclaiming the faith for which he longed, Wesley eventually discovered it.

When I apply this to myself, I realise that the hymns I sing help me to dive into the 'deep end' of the Gospel and, as I luxuriate there in its warmth, I am enveloped by its wonders. It is as I celebrate the Christian Perfection that I seek, that the Holy Spirit draws me towards my goal. So I will keep on singing about the blessings God has yet to complete in me.

The Preacher's final instruction is, "Respect and obey God".

I prefer the *NIV*'s "Stand in awe of God".

There is a profound need for mystery in religious faith. When I go to church I want to feel that I am caught up in something eternal and rare. It is my moment on the Transfiguration Mount when I "breathe a purer air."

Is it any wonder that cathedrals and new 'community' churches have growing congregations when, in their different ways, they offer 'wonder'? Whether the setting is soaring mediaeval glory or joyous, charismatic excitement, worshippers are caught up in something awesome and exhilarating.

I do realise that, on Sundays, even our plain little Methodist chapel can be transformed into 'the House of an awesome God'. Therefore, its worship may be simple but it must never be mundane or shoddy. We must never do less than 'worship the Lord in the beauty of Holiness.'

O worship the Lord in the beauty of holiness!
Bow down before Him, His glory proclaim;
With gold of obedience and incense of lowliness,
Kneel and adore Him, the Lord is His name.
Fear not to enter His courts in the slenderness
Of the poor wealth thou wouldst reckon as thine;
Truth in its beauty and love in its tenderness,
These are the offerings to lay on His shrine.

John Samuel Monsell (1811-75)

TODAY'S RESOLVE

Today I will 'swim out of my depth'. I will read two great hymns which describe the kind of spiritual experience to which I aspire.

PRAYER

Magnificent and awesome Lord, as I read, give me a glimpse of your greatness and of your intention for my life. Amen.

9: "THE MIDDLE OF THE ROAD"

Reading: Eccl 7:15-25   (Key: Verses 16 & 18)

"Don't destroy yourself by being too good...keep to the middle of the road."

I haven't time to linger over the insights in Chapter 6 but I really can't walk past this incredible piece of advice! Is it really possible that trying to 'be too good' can destroy me? Surely, I ought always to strive for the best and I know that walking in the middle of the road merely invites accidents! Nevertheless, the idea nags and will not go away. I think that I understand what he means. I still love the old, *Order of Morning Prayer* we used in College Chapel but I remember feeling that repenting of the same sins every morning in *The General Confession* smacked of spiritual defeatism

However, there is a kind of religion which cherishes its 'miserable offenders' badge and never expects or allows the burden of sin and guilt to be lifted. Its devotees seem intent upon committing spiritual suicide. They are destroyed by their fervent and frustrated attempts to be 'good'. I remember reading some solemn words by an eminent Victorian clergyman. Revd. George Dawson cautioned his readers against living a 'life too mirthful'. Surely that can't be right.

By a providential coincidence! I have just been reading an article entitled *The Poison of Perfectionism* in which the writer describes the spiritual and psychological dangers of demanding excessively high standards for ourselves and for others in the church. He warns me that, when I am unable to achieve these unreasonable demands, I can destroy myself with guilt and others by my criticism.

On the other hand, am I to say that sin doesn't matter? Is God an indulgent old gentleman who simply smiles benignly at the peccadilloes of his wayward children? I know that Jesus may not have talked much about sin but he took it seriously enough to die so that he could defeat it. No! I have to take sin seriously. Is there, then, some genuine 'middle way' between spiritual pessimism and the antinomians who tell me that, since I am saved by faith alone, I can do whatever I like." I half remember some enigmatic words by Maggie Ross in *The Fountain and the Furnace,* "Sin both matters terribly and matters not at all". I think that I am beginning to understand what she meant.

First of all, I must take Jesus' offer of forgiveness at least as seriously as I take my own sin. If he says to me, as he said to the paralytic, "Your sins are forgiven", I must believe that he is telling the truth. He is not a liar. Moreover, his forgiveness is not a single act of absolution, it is a process, a 'seventy times seven' cleansing of my sin every day. I don't know how Jesus can have such patience with me but he does. Sin 'does not have dominion over me'. As my Kenyan friends used to say, "I am cleansed in the blood of the Lamb."

Secondly, I am realistic about my sin but that does not mean that I cannot step out confidently in the footsteps of a Lord whose intention for me is 'eternal life'. For me, the bells of faith do not toll a single knell of doom but a joyous 'grandsire triple' peal of hope.

I remember presiding at a 'Sankey Evening' in Cornwall. The sheer glory of the singing made my sparse hair stand on end as hundreds of Methodists proclaimed that they were "marching to Zion". It is in that hymn that Isaac Watts has a memorable couplet which sums up what I need to re-learn,

Religion never was designed
To make our pleasures less.

Of course he is right! My faith is not intended to plunge me into ever greater depths of misery of guilt. It is intended to increase my zest for living. Jesus says that following him is about being 'blessed' and 'joyful'. It is about 'abundant life' and divine friendship. A miserable Christian is a heretic of the worst kind!
Come, ye that love the Lord,
And let your joys be known;
Join in a song with sweet accord,
While ye surround the throne:
Let those refuse to sing
Who never knew our God;
But servants of the heavenly King
May speak their joys abroad.

Isaac Watts (1674-88)

TODAY'S RESOLVE
Even if it is a 'difficult' day, I will make a short list of the things that God has given me to make me happy and I will thank God for them.

PRAYER
Loving Lord, show me your authentic 'middle way' so that I can acknowledge my sins under the umbrella of your wonderful forgiveness. Amen

10: "BREAD ON WATER"

Reading: Eccl 11: 1-6   **(Key: Verse 1)**

"Cast your bread upon the waters, for you will find it after many days.

It's a bit like coming home from a holiday before I have had time to see all the local attractions but the time has come to leave. I can't spend the whole of Lent in *Ecclesiastes.* There are other places to go and other sights to see but, before I leave, there is just one last verse to visit.

Towards the end of his book The Preacher becomes all mysterious and bombards me with 'dark sayings' and the first of them has grabbed my attention. I will keep the Key Verse in the King James Version because it sounds suitably enigmatic.

Of all the scholars' endless arguments about its interpretation, there is one that seems to me to make most sense. In ancient Egypt, farmers would throw seeds into the River Nile while it was in flood. Then they had to wait until the waters receded and the seeds had sunk into the rich silt to give them their harvest.

But still the puzzle isn't solved. There are two very different modern paraphrases. The first says, "Don't be afraid to invest. Someday it will pay off" which sounds like a bugle-call to courageous living. To be honest, I'm not a particularly 'courageous' Christian.

I like to weigh up the *pros and cons* before I make a move. If I had been one of the first disciples, I am sure that I would have asked lots of questions before giving up the family business. Not for me 'leaving everything and following Jesus' just like that!

However, looking back over my life, whenever I **have** responded to a Spirit-impulse and done something 'stupid' for Jesus, eventually the dividends have been wonderful. So why on earth don't I always do it automatically? Is it because I have imbibed the spirit of the age and refuse to obey my Lord unless he can guarantee me fast-tracked blessings? Anyway, I need to hear The Preacher's advice,

The other paraphrase is, "Be generous and someday you will be rewarded." Oddly, I see that our word 'generous' comes from a Latin word meaning 'well born' because noble and wealthy Roman citizens were expected to give liberally to the poor. This makes me think. If the 'well born' were expected to be generous, what about those who are 'born again'?

Through Jesus I have received the incredible gift of 'new life' but I must not keep the blessing for myself. As Peter reminds me, "Each of us has been blessed with one of God's wonderful gifts to be used in the service of others." (*I Peter* 4.10) Generosity must be part of my spiritual DNA.

However, what about "someday you will be rewarded"? It's that 'someday' that I don't like. I want people to be immediately grateful when I do something kind. If they seem ungrateful, what is my reaction? "It wouldn't hurt them to say 'thank you'. Well, I won't be helping *them* next time!" I conveniently forget how ungrateful I can be, even to the people to whom I owe most.

But, even more, I should be troubled by my ingratitude to God. Have I given God the gratitude of perfect obedience? No! So has God said to me, "It wouldn't hurt David to say 'thank you'. I won't be helping *him* next time."? No, God has not!

I'll sing of the 'Lord's everlasting mercies' *(Psalm 100:4),* and try to copy God's wonderful generosity,

Finally, I thank the Preacher for letting me travel with him. I have learned valuable lessons on the road.

To give and give and give again
What God hath given thee;
To spend thyself nor count the cost,
To serve right gloriously
The God who gave all worlds that are,
And all that are to be.
                    Geoffrey Studdert-Kennedy (1993-1929)

TODAY'S RESOLVE
I will try to be generous to somebody who I know cannot or will not thank me – just so that I get into the 'giving' habit.

PRAYER
        Generous God, forgive my constant ingratitude and help me to copy your generosity and to be a blessing to others. Amen.

11: "JUDE THE OBSCURE"

Reading: Jude vv. 1-8   **(Key: Verse 1)**

"To all who are chosen and loved by God the Father and are kept safe by Jesus Christ."

This is a much shorter 'Bible by-way' than *Ecclesiastes*, less than thirty verses long. I'd miss it altogether if two pages of my Bible were to stick together. Neglected alike by preachers and Bible readers, it only scraped into the New Testament by the skin of its teeth. Indeed, like Thomas Hardy's sad hero, it is *Jude the Obscure.*

I am told that it is a little like a Manchester church which bears Jude's name. Although it is an architectural 'little gem' standing in the city centre, most people pass it by without a second glance. Yet, I have found that reading *Jude* carefully is like discovering that what I had thought was a 50p 'car boot sale' trinket is actually a priceless jewel.

If it is written by "the brother of James" who was "the Lord's brother" (*Galatians* 1:19), it must be very special. Once, one of Jesus' unbelieving brothers, (*John* 7:1-9), Jude is now a revered church leader and I need to hear him. He offers me three blessings.

Firstly, he explains to me what a great privilege it is to be a Christian.

To be honest, sometimes, I catch myself thinking that I have done Jesus a good turn by choosing to serve him. He should be grateful that I have decided to favour him with my 'custom'! Jude corrects my arrogant stupidity and tells me that the only reason that I am even **allowed** to be a Christian is because God has permitted it. As Jesus himself says, "You did not choose me. I chose you." (*John* 15:16)

Next, Jude takes my breath away by telling me that it is *God the Father* who has 'chosen and loved me.'

I'm 'breathless' because I have this huge problem. How can the Maker of Black Holes and Parallel Universes know anything about little me, let alone 'love' me? I know that if I, a mere human, can love many people, Infinite Love can embrace all its children but, even so, when I try to reason it out, I find, like Lear, 'that way madness lies'. I can only cling to the cross. There, in a way that I am able to understand, I see the lengths to which that Divine Love which cascades heaven with billions of stars will go to 'choose and love' me. I just have to accept it in breathless wonder.

However, I've just seen that some ancient versions say that God has 'chosen and **sanctified**' me.

What a remarkable idea! In the Bible, 'sanctified and 'holy' places and objects are set apart for God's special use and Jude is saying that I am separated in this world for a special purpose. As Jesus says, "I chose you out of the world." (John 17:19). But, wait a moment; I am not 'out of the world'. I am still in 'the world' with all its mess of cruelty, violence and sheer wickedness! How can I possibly survive and be 'holy'?

This is where my third blessing comes in.

Jude says, that I am 'kept safe by Jesus Christ'. He calms me and says, "You can safely swim in the sea without getting drowned and you can live in the world without being destroyed by it." Jesus will alert me when I risk being swept into temptation and give me strength to swim back to the shore of 'sanctified living'.

Yes, *Jude* is, indeed, a gem, but no longer **hidden** for us!

What is our calling's glorious hope
But inward holiness?
For this to Jesus I look up,
I calmly wait for this.
From all iniquity, from all,
He shall my soul redeem;
In Jesus I believe and shall
Believe myself to Him.

Charles Wesley (1707-88)

TODAY'S RESOLVE
I will be humbly proud of being a Christian and I will not hide it from anybody I meet.

PRAYER
Lord Jesus, forgive my pride and cowardice and help me today to give a clear but winsome witness to my friends, family and colleagues. Amen.

12: "TORTOISE CHRISTIANS"

Reading: Jude vv.1-4.   **(Key: Verse 3)**

"I write to ask you to defend the faith which god has once for all given to his people."

I have a sneaking admiration for old Dr. Bowdler, the 19th Century physician who surgically removed the 'saucy' bits from Shakespeare's *Works* so that Victorian families might read them without blushing. I think that this translation of the text has received a 'Bowdler' touch because, if my fallible Greek serves me, this is no polite request. Jude's words are much stronger. "Keep on fighting like mad to defend the faith!" My thoughts about this will get me into trouble but here goes! I am not a very bellicose man but I pray for the return of 'fighting mad' Christians!

I can remember sitting in Sunday School listening to my saintly teacher's carefully-prepared lessons but all the time I was longing to sing *Onward Christian Soldiers, Fight the Good Fight and Stand up, Stand up for Jesus* to lift the tedium. (Ungrateful little wretch that I was!) But where are those stirring hymns now? Bowdlerized! Expunged from modern hymnbooks, as embarrassing reminders of an Imperialist Age, and 'muscular Christianity'.

I understand why this has happened and why references to 'fighting' have almost disappeared from modern hymns. I know about Victorian Christian' Rule Britannia' jingoism and, of course, I appreciate that

Jesus forbade his followers to fight like the armies of earthly kingdoms. I know that Christians must stand against the violence which is ripping the guts out of the world. I see helpless Christians driven from the Middle East, and cry with the Psalmist, *How long, O Lord, How long?* All this I know but, nevertheless, another thought insistently bores itself into my mind. Does all this mean that my faith is expected to be totally non-combative?

Is my Christianity intended to have the consistency of blancmange? Is the destiny of Christians simply to 'go with the flow', to forgive everybody for everything and just get on with running food-banks and charities? No! Paul is right! I may not 'wrestle against flesh and blood' but I do 'contend against spiritual wickedness in high places' and need to invest in the whole armour of God' (*Ephesians* 6:12). I need the finest equipment for the fight.

I grew up in a Britain where most of our neighbours called themselves 'Christians' and many made at least an annual pilgrimage to church. Now, that is no longer true. Those who claim to be Christians are a shrinking minority and regular churchgoers are a dying breed (literally!). Aggressive atheism kidnaps the minds of young people and Christian 'rights' are increasingly suffocated by a secularist state. Whether I like it or not I am caught up in a fierce spiritual conflict. There is an urgent need for contemporary Christians to start 'fighting like mad to defend the faith'.

When the Great War began, few in Britain took it seriously because nobody believed how dangerous the situation had become. Everybody said that it would be 'over by Christmas'. Is that happening in today's spiritual warfare? I can't help thinking of that parody of the hymn, "*Like a mighty army moves the Church of God*",

Like a mighty tortoise moves the Church of God
Brothers, we are treading where we've always trod.

'Tortoise Christians' – now there's an idea! There are Christians who seldom peep out from under their protective 'churchy' shell to see what's happening in the world. Am I being alarmist in wanting to disturb them? Have I any alternative but, to be like a latter-day Jude and sing out loud to Christians who are in denial?

Stand up, stand up for Jesus!
Stand in His strength alone:
The arm of flesh will fail you;
Ye dare not trust your own.
Put on the Christian's armour,
And watching on to prayer,
Where duty calls, or danger,
Be never wanting there.

George Duffield (1818-88)

TODAY'S RESOLVE
Today, if there is an opportunity to defend the faith, I will seize it and not apologise.

PRAYER
Lord, I don't find it easy to speak up and defend my faith. Help me when the opportunity comes not to avoid speaking up and out. Amen.

13: "3D-EVIL"

Reading: Jude vv. 3-4   **(Key: Verse 4)**

"Some godless people have sneaked in among us."

I see that Jude says that he has had to change his plans. He has replaced his intended letter "about God's saving work" by an emergency tract. The reason is that, 'godless people' have infiltrated the church in Syrian Antioch. As he describes their sinister activities, I find an echo of my own experience and, almost unwittingly, I have preached myself a three-point sermon! Obviously old preachers never die!

Like Churchill's definition of Russia, Evil is "a riddle wrapped in a mystery inside an enigma" so, for practical purposes, I find it easier to personify it as The Devil (but hereafter I won't dignify that being with a capital initial!) For me, this passage from *Jude* raises three red warning flags over the devil.

Firstly, as Jesus warned, by nature, evil uses **deception** and, like true apprentices of 'the father of lies', these false teachers do everything 'according to his book'.

They 'sneak in'. This rings bells for me. I seldom find that the devil makes a frontal assault. Instead, he tries to outflank me, creeping up on my blind side. He sneaks in so silently that I scarcely notice that he is there. Then, because I think that I'm safe and secure, I relax – and he pounces! It is then that I can be defeated.

There is another aspect of Jude's problem that I find familiar. The devil's apprentices come **in disguise** - and in just the right disguise too.

They come as *bona fide* teachers. Keen to learn, those Antiochene Christians will welcome the insights of new 'teachers'. O how I wish that the devil still came to me as a Mediaeval black, horned monster! But he doesn't. He comes in disguise and he won't waste his time using people I can't stand. He will come to me in the guise of people I find attractive and persuasive. I can't forget that it was his friend Simon Peter, whom Jesus called 'Satan'! I think of some embarrassing occasions when I have accepted bad advice largely because I have liked the advisor. So why have I given in so easily?

This is where the devil's third characteristic comes in. He is **desirable.**

He tells me what I want to hear. True to form, the devil's apprentices assure the listening Christians that God overlooks immorality. The devil knows exactly where to strike. Like seaports all over the world, Syrian Antioch was a wild place and Christian converts there would have had to give up plenty of their former vices. What more desirable news could they want to hear? "You can go back to your old ways with God's blessing!"

This is arrant nonsense, but it is so alluring. If I accept it and stroll complacently along life's broad and easy path, I can be sure that the devil is grinning at me from behind the hedge!

Evil is intelligent and, although grosser Antiochene vices no longer appeal to me, it will use more subtle 'desirable' temptations - pride, self-centredness, touchiness and the like.

Whenever I hear a beguiling voice wooing me to lower my Christian standards, I need Jude's urgent warning. To surrender to whisperings of 3D-Evil is to "deny that I must obey Jesus Christ as my only Master." There is no room for compromise,

Fain would we cease from sinning
In thought, and word, and deed;
From sin in its beginning
We languish to be freed;
From every base desire,
Our fallen nature's shame,
Jesus, we dare require
Deliverance in Thy name.

Charles Wesley (1707-88)

TODAY'S RESOLVE
Today I will watch the weak-spots in my character and make sure that they are not exploited by subtle temptations.

PRAYER
Lord Jesus, who outwitted the devil in the desert; give me your awareness to detect the approach of evil and to defeat it in your name. Amen.

14: "CURIOSER AND CURIOSER!"

Reading: Jude vv. 5-9   **(Key: Verses 8-9)**

"Even Michael, the chief angel, didn't dare to insult the devil, when the two of them were arguing about the body of Moses, all that Michael said was, 'the Lord will rebuke you!'"

I can't ignore it! My curiosity has been thoroughly aroused. Obviously, this was a well-known old legend which told how the devil tried to seize Moses' hidden grave (*Deuteronomy* 34:6) from its guardian, the Archangel Michael. Although Michael is horrified by such wickedness, he has respect for Satan as a fellow-angel (albeit a fallen one) and he refuses to retaliate, leaving Satan's punishment to God. It is an odd story and I react to it rather like Alice in Wonderland when "she was so surprised that she quite forgot how to speak good English". "Curiouser and curiouser!"

It has set my mind off in an unexpected direction. What a wonderful, powerful thing *curiosity* is!

I think that it was Einstein who said that curiosity "has its own reason for existence." Isn't it amazing that the same human curiosity that made me research this legend also fuelled the Theory of Relativity and the quest for the Higgs Boson? I have never thought before of the power of curiosity in the spiritual life but it's so obvious. Why haven't I noticed it long ago?

I've read that Mother Teresa once counselled her nuns "to avoid curiosity" but who can come to faith except through the door of Spirit-fired curiosity? Is it impudent to think that those feisty young fishermen responded to Jesus' enigmatic "Follow me" because they were *curious*? Where would Jesus lead them? What would they do? And it was not only the first disciples. I think of that little miser up a tree. Whatever made Zacchaeus do such an undignified thing? It was *curiosity*! He 'wanted to see Jesus' and it saved his soul. What about the curious crowds flocking to hear Jesus, the Greeks 'wanting to see' him, Nicodemus coming to him by night? Church history is crammed with stories of people whose curiosity initially drew them to the Gospel.

However, it is more than the initial encounter with Jesus Christ that is involved here. It is by exercising spiritual curiosity that I grow in grace and understanding. Occasionally, I have met Christians who make a virtue of godly inertia. They appear to remain spiritually static and their faith sits upon them like a cold pancake. Is it because they are terrified by their own curiosity? Are they afraid to ask big questions lest the answers wreck their faith? What a pity!

I remember a lovely sermon illustration by the great 19th Century Scottish divine, Robert McCheyne. He said that being a Christian is like standing on the prow of a ship and looking out over God's love, 'a vast circle of ocean without any bound'. I have a divine commission to sail far and wide in that ocean following the compass of my curiosity. Sometimes it may lead me into troubled waters but, guided by the Spirit, I will never flounder and sink.

A rather portly well-off industrialist was invited to dinner and came under the curiosity-filled gaze of the young lad of the household. "What are you looking at?" questioned the visitor. "My parents told me that you are a self-made man and I wanted to see what you looked like", replied the boy. "Ah yes, preened the industrialist, I am a self-made man!" "What did you make yourself like that for", was the boy's response. A question that we may all need to answer for ourselves! I wish that my life was so visibly Christ-like that it would make people curious about my Lord. Ah well!

Fill Thou my life, O Lord my God,
In every part with praise,
That my whole being may proclaim
Thy being and Thy ways
Praise in the common things of life,
Its goings out and in;
Praise in each duty and each deed,
However small and mean.
Fill every part of me with praise;
Let all my being speak
Of Thee and of Thy love, O Lord,
Poor though I be and weak.

Horatius Bonar (1808-89)

TODAY'S RESOLVE

Today, I will be curious about just one of life's big questions and will do some more thinking about it.

PRAYER

Mysterious God, you have given so many big questions to stimulate my curiosity. Help me to explore them and patiently to wait as the Holy Spirit increases my understanding. Amen

15: "GOODIES AND BADDIES"

Reading: Jude vv. 10-16   **(Key: Verse 12)**

"These people are filthy minded, and by their shameful and selfish actions, they spoil the meals you eat together."

Jude really 'pulls out all the stops' in attacking the false teachers. They are 'godless Christ-deniers', 'senseless animals', 'murdering money-grabbers', 'rainless clouds', 'leafless trees', 'wandering stars' and 'braggarts' worthy of the terrible punishment prophesied by the mysterious Enoch.

Is there another New Testament passage where so many condemnatory metaphors are hurled in so short a space of time? Jude allows these 'godless people' no hint of goodness.

This has made me think. Are people really like that – 'good' or 'bad'? Isn't it possible that these teachers, these 'wandering stars', didn't see themselves as 'godless people'? Perhaps they honestly believed that God had sent them to save Antiochene Christians from joy-stifling puritanism. After all, they might have argued, the great Paul taught that good works don't save us, so why claim that they are so all-important? Perhaps they had a point! Horror of horrors! I'm beginning to like these people! They may have had some wrong ideas but that doesn't mean that they had no good qualities.

What an eye-opener this is about conflicts in churches! Christians who are supposed to be good at forgiving their enemies are often not very good at forgiving their friends. Fortunately, it has been a rare occurrence in my ministry but I have seen it happen in church councils when divisive issues are discussed.

Disagreement has led to demonizing. Each combatant has thought, "I am speaking out of the finest altruistic Christian concern for the welfare of this church but he (or she) is being deliberately evil and obstructive. I always knew that they were devious and underhand!" In no time, old friends have become new enemies and the fellowship is sundered.

When I joined my rowdy boyhood friends on the front row of the Saturday morning cinema, we could tell the 'goodies' from the 'baddies' by the colour of their hats. Films were straightforward contests between good and evil presented in a thousand different variations.

However, they tell me that, today, some films are blurring the lines as villains are given great virtues and heroes are accorded great flaws. *Peter Pan's* Captain Hook and *Oz's* Wicked Witch of the West are given a new, disarming moral facelift.

Perhaps the Church (and that includes me) has a lesson to learn from the cinema. Life is not a simple contest between 'goodies' and 'baddies'.

Heretics can have precious insights and troublemakers can speak rare truths.

Instead of dismissing them, I should listen to them. Instead of demonizing them I should remember that Jesus died to redeem even those who seem to have few redeeming qualities.

Let us join- 'tis God commands-
Let us join our hearts and hands;
Help to gain our calling's hope,
Build we each the other up:
Still forget the things behind,
Follow Christ in heart and mind,
Towards the mark unwearied press,
Seize the crown of righteousness.
While we walk with God in light,
God our hearts doth still unite;
Dearest fellowship we prove,
Fellowship in Jesu's love.

Charles Wesley (1707-88)

TODAY'S RESOLVE
I will think of somebody I find 'difficult' and deliberately celebrate their good qualities.

PRAYER
Loving Lord, help me to handle disagreements better and to remember that you give different truths to different people. Amen

16: "A MOBILE GOD "

Reading: Jude vv. 17-23   (Key: Verses 20-21)

"Dear friends ..... keep in step with God's love, as you wait for our lord Jesus Christ ...."

Jude and his friends expected the Second Coming to happen very soon but, meanwhile, they simply had to wait. I am not a very good 'waiter'.

To me, it is one of the mysteries of the universe that clocks in Waiting Rooms always seem to run at half-speed. Waiting-time seems double time.

Nevertheless, Jude's readers are told that they must wait and that the waiting will be of a special kind. It is to be *active* waiting which is why these verses seem to bounce along with words like 'build', 'help', 'rescue' and 'have mercy'.

I'm aware that, as I have grown older, I have become more tempted to rest by the wayside. I don't have the energy to run spiritual marathons as once I did. Sleep seems increasingly attractive.

For some odd reason (perhaps because I've been 'doing a bit of Shakespeare' recently) I am remembering Oberon dripping magic juice into Titania's sleeping eyes so that she wakes to fall in love with the asinine Bottom.

It's a sort of parable for me. I realise that if I succumb to alluring spiritual slumber, I too will awake with my vision distorted. I will begin to think that my God has finished with me and that I can comfortably nestle down and fade away.

Jude reminds me that my Lord has no spiritual Chelsea Pensioners living in well-deserved retirement. I like the translation 'keep in step with God's love'. It conjures up a picture of a God who is always active, always creating, always working.

Not for me the god of the Deists who winds up his universe and then sinks into eternal slumber. I remember boyhood country rambles with my parents. I always seemed to walk much better when my little legs tried to keep pace with my father's longer strides.

It is because my loving Heavenly Father is calling me to 'keep up' that I cannot be content with my present Christian life. He has more places for me to go, more discoveries for me to make. Perhaps they will be less familiar landscapes - the meadows of more reflection, prayer, study and caring but, wherever God leads me, I must keep in step.

It doesn't matter if I can't make long term plans as once I did. I am committed to *activity in waiting* until the time when I'm finally called home.

Each day is a new walk with God and God always has a diurnal destination in mind for me. Sometimes that destination is clear and important; sometimes it is unclear and quite ordinary.

But of one thing I can be sure, no day is pointless when I am "keeping in step with God's love."

If on our daily course our mind
Be set to hallow all we find,
New treasures still of countless price,
God will provide for sacrifice.
Old friends, old scenes will lovelier be;
As more of heaven in each we see;
Some softening gleam of love and prayer
Shall dawn on every cross and care.

John Keble (1792-1866)

TODAY'S RESOLVE

I will not let today pass without having achieved something, great or small, for Jesus.

PRAYER

Dear Lord, I'm not very good at discerning your will. Please show me what you want to do with me today. Amen.

17: "FLYING HIGH"

Reading: Jude vv.24-25   (Key: Verses 24-25)

"Now unto Him that is able to keep you from falling and to present you faultless before the presence of his glory. To the only wise God our Saviour be glory and majesty, devotion and power both now and forever. Amen."

I can't think of this wonderful Ascription except in the KJV. To update it seems almost sacrilegious.

In various forms it must be used hundreds of times every Sunday but I wonder how many people know its origin. I'm surprised to find that Jude's tract, so full of earthy condemnation, ends with such a sublime vision of the believer standing before the glory of God.

A recent magnificent performance of Elgar's *Dream of Gerontius* is indelibly imprinted upon my memory. It was literally elevating! How amazing to be present as Gerontius' soul floats free with 'an inexpressive lightness' to enjoy a momentary sight of Christ in glory before sinking into the cleansing waters of Purgatory. I reject Newman's purgatorial theology but, for a couple of hours, he and Elgar had me exploring heaven. They rebuked my theology for being so horribly cumbersome and earthbound! Why is it that I scarcely ever think about heaven?

Perhaps I fear the old charge of being "so heavenly minded that I'm no earthly use" but Jude reminds me that it is just as bad to be being 'so earthly-minded that I'm no heavenly use'.

I hear Paul telling me that, "If in this life only I have hope in Christ, I am of all men most miserable." (*I Cor.* 15:19) Faith that feels no desire for 'the presence of his glory' is a poor, fiddling earth-bound state.

Recently, I listened to some astro-physicists talking about working on the frontiers of human reason and gazing into mystery and I began to wonder if they were not today's true theologians! They really understand how magnificent our creator God must be.

So what am I saying to myself? I have read enough of the mystics' writings to know that I am not naturally one of them but, on the other hand, I may be making God too 'manageable'.

I need to redress the balance by launching out into those areas of faith where my native reason is ill at ease.

Why not read again the works of those great spiritual writers who seem to exist at a spiritual altitude which makes me gasp? Why not concentrate upon studying the visionary passages of Scripture? Why not try new ways of prayer? Why not talk to Christians whose spiritual experience is different from my own?

Thank you, Jude, for making me think 'outside the box'!

Give me the wings of faith to rise
Within the veil, and see
The saints above, how great their joys,
How bright their glories be.
I ask them whence their victory came;
They, with united breath,
Ascribe their conquest to the Lamb,
Their triumph to His death.

Isaac Watts (1674-1748)

TODAY'S RESOLVE
I will read slowly some hymns and poems about heaven and let them speak to me.

PRAYER
Lord, forgive me for trying to domesticate you and make you little. Show me ways that I can reach into the 'presence of your glory'. Amen.

ZEPHANIAH

DAY EIGHTEEN

18: "A DORIAN GRAY SOCIETY"

Reading: Zephaniah Chapter One   (Key: Verse 18)

"Not even your silver or gold can save you on that day when I the Lord am angry"

Whenever I have opened *Zephaniah* (which I have to admit has not been very often) it has felt like walking along a dark path with overarching trees and dark bushes. I understand why the prophet is so gloomy. He must tell his people that, because of their sins, the doom they covet for their enemies is also going to fall on them. This is not the news they want to hear, especially when it is told with such apparent relish.

Yet the Key Verse has emerged from the gloom to make me ponder. I don't like to think of God being angry, because the only kind of anger I know is my own bubbling brew of self-preservation and pride. However, I know that God cannot simply ignore the evil in his world.

Perhaps that is why I still prefer the old word 'wrath'. It seems to me to represent God's pure and implacable opposition to evil wherever it is found. However, it is an arresting idea that Zephaniah identifies the rich as the specific objects of God's anger. These are the people who have done well economically and who think that, consequently, they are 'bomb proof'.

59

I have a strong feeling that this scenario is being re-enacted in our own times but to the nth. degree. Perhaps people are no more evil now than they were in the past but something sinister is happening in our society.

It reminds me of Oscar Wilde's, story of young man who is seduced into a life of sinful degradation. *The Picture of Dorian Gray* scandalized polite Victorian society because, in spite of his debauchery, its 'hero' never shows any overt signs of aging or self-indulgence. He is immune to the effects of his vices because, hidden in his house; there is a portrait of him which miraculously bears all the disfiguring marks of his growing age and depravity. The outside world sees only a handsome, successful young buck but, all the time, his true self is withering in his attic.

For me, this has become a sort of picture parable of the world today. Sadly, I see so many people around me who seem to pour all their energy into physical, material things and appear to thrive on it. Apparently, they are successful and content but, hidden from view they have lost sight of their Spiritual Selves, their Real Selves, their Eternal Selves, and their God-contacting Selves which are withering away through neglect. Truly, it means that they are only half alive because, for most of the time, their more important part of being has been forgotten.

Oscar Wilde's story ends in tragedy when Dorian Gray has to face the truth about himself and, slashing his portrait with a knife, he dies a wizened, shrunken, sin-raddled horror. It is a parable for modern times. It is fatal to neglect one's spiritual self.

Perhaps this is how the 'wrath of God' works. Perhaps, if we are determined to destroy ourselves, reluctantly, He permits us to do so.

So what is the message for me? As a Christian, it is my task to awaken others to the reality and importance of their unseen Spiritual Selves. I must do this skilfully and humbly with no sense of being superior or 'holier than thou'.

I must sincerely want others to experience the thrill and joy of discovering that part of them that can feel the presence of God. It is delicate soul-surgery and I must use a scalpel not a hatchet. Only God himself can give me the skill and patience that I need.

Enthrone thy God within thy heart,
Thy being's inmost shrine;
He doth to thee the power impart
To live the life divine.
Seek truth in Him with Christlike mind;
With faith His will discern;
Walk on life's way with him and find
Thy heart within thee burn.

W.J. Penn (1875-1956)

TODAY'S RESOLVE

I will look for an opportunity to have a spiritual conversation with somebody

PRAYER

Lord, I am so unskilled in my attempts to awaken others to their spirituality, please give me the confidence to try and then overcome my inadequacy by your grace. Amen

PHILEMON

DAY NINETEEN

19: "PAUL'S POSTCARD"

Reading: The Letter to Philemon   (Key: Verse 16)

"Onesimus is much more than a slave.....he is a follower of the Lord."

Today I am wandering along one of the prettiest of the Bible's by-ways. It's not so much a letter as a large postcard – less than 350 Greek words. It makes no great theological statements and carries no instructions for wayward congregations.

At first sight, The Letter to Philemon is simply a request from one friend to another. The imprisoned Paul is pleading the cause of Onesimus, a runaway slave, who has been living with him in Rome. Now, repentantly, Onesimus wants to return to his master Philemon, a wealthy Colossian Christian and Paul begs Philemon to receive him.

However, the more I think about it, the more I realise what a potential tragedy lies behind this lovely letter. Paul is asking the seemingly impossible. If I think of it as a set of scales, one side is loaded down with everything that might go wrong.

To begin with, Onesimus is not only a runaway but a thief and so has little to recommend him to his master's mercy.

Then, Philemon may do his civic duty and inform the authorities that Paul has been harbouring a runaway slave, which would incur severe penalties.

Thirdly, there is a very good chance that Onesimus will never reach Philemon safely. Colossae is a long way from Rome and, even with Tychicus as his companion; he might well be seized *en route* by the dreaded slave-hunting *fugitivari*.

Finally, even if Onesimus arrives safely, Philemon is perfectly within his legal rights to brand his forehead with red-hot irons, scourge him and even crucify him.

What is placed on the other side of the scales? Only Paul's trust in Philemon's Christian forgiveness. That is what this letter is all about - the amazing quality of true Christian forgiveness and it has made me think.

Every day I pray, "Forgive my trespasses as I forgive those that trespass against me" and I think that I have done well if I have managed to forgive a few petty annoyances. But that is not the range of true Christian forgiveness.

True Christian forgiveness is 'Onesimus forgiveness' – the blotting out of some terrible outrage which rightly makes me furious. Christian forgiveness is 'Calvary forgiveness'. It is 'Father-forgive-them-for-they-know-not-what-they-do- forgiveness', which even prays from the Cross for the crucifiers.

.

I have never had to exercise that kind of forgiveness and I am by no means certain that I have it in me to do so if it were truly tested. I need to be invaded afresh by the love of Christ. Back to prayer!

Jesus, thine all-victorious love,
Shed in my heart abroad;
Then shall my feet no longer rove,
Rooted and fixed in God.
Refining fire, go through my heart,
Illuminate my soul;
Scatter Thy life through every part,
And sanctify the whole.

Charles Wesley (1707-88)

TODAY'S RESOLVE
Today, I will remember the times when other people have forgiven me and then I will remember anyone I need to forgive and do it gladly.

PRAYER
Loving Lord, I live each day by your forgiveness, help me to cultivate an ability to forgive little annoyances so that, if I ever I need to exercise big forgiveness I will be better prepared. Amen.

DAY TWENTY

20: "IMPATIENT WITH GOD"

Reading: Habakkuk 1:1-4   **(Key: Verse 2)**

"O Lord, how long must I beg for your help before you listen?"

This truly is a Bible 'B Road'. I have to confess that my Bible does not automatically fall open at *Habakkuk*. In fact, I've had to remind myself that he was probably a prophet/priest writing in Judah's dark days before the Babylonian invasion. His name probably means "One who clings to God" and it suits the cry of desperation that opens his book. He looks around and sees only violence, injustice, lawlessness, crime and cruelty and pleads with God to do something about it.

I know a little of how he feels! From almost every corner of the globe, my television bombards me with just the same horrors – and God seems to do nothing about it! Of course, I know that it is people like me who cause the problems and that we have a God-given ability to put things right. Nevertheless, I still expect Him to intervene and, when I list these horrors in my prayers, I sometimes have a dull sense of hopelessness. I wish that Habakkuk had not reminded me of my dilemma. However, now I can't avoid trying to make some sense of it. There is one thing of which I am absolutely sure. God is good and there is no situation for which God has not already provided a solution. So why doesn't God *do* something! All sorts of ideas whirl around in my mind.

One ray of understanding comes. I must accept that only God knows the complexity of any particular issue. For me, situations tend to appear as clear options between right and wrong but God knows that that is seldom true. On both sides there are people who think that they are well-intentioned and nobody has all the truth. How wisely Jesus spoke of the need to allow weeds and wheat to grow together until harvest!

It follows that correcting one problem may simply compound greater problems elsewhere. I remember two grainy First World War photographs showing British and German chaplains standing before their rival armies praying for victory. Since God loves all his children, whose prayer is God to answer when God knows that victory for one side simply means disaster for the other? What does Love do?

Then, what about timing? Perhaps God delays because it is too soon to act. Perhaps circumstances must change. There may be a thousand reasons why God is saying, 'Not yet'. I know from experience that whenever I have been impatient and moved too quickly, I have always regretted it. Another idea has just come to me. Often there is no single solution to a problem. Perhaps various parties have to be ready to change. I like Robert Louis Stevenson's homespun wisdom, "Compromise is the best and cheapest lawyer." How many intractable conflicts eventually have had to end in compromise but, sadly, only after much blood has been shed!

But let me bring this to my own doormat. When I cry out, "Lord, how long?" What then? With Martin Luther, I must "Let God be God!" I must accept that I may not know why God delays but **God knows!** I know that, whatever the answer may be it will never be because God does not care – Jesus on the Cross shows me that! It is a matter of trust but there is something more. Sometimes God wants to use me to help improve the situation because I may even be part of the problem!

To be brutally honest, next time I see starving children or victims of genocide, I'm afraid that all my 'clever' ideas about 'unanswered' prayer will sound uncomfortably trite but it's the best I can do. I can only be like Habakkuk and 'cling to God'.

Blest are the saints of God,
That stay themselves on Thee!
Who wait for Thy salvation, Lord,
Shall Thy salvation see.
When we in darkness walk,
Nor feel the heavenly flame,
Then is the time to trust our God
And rest upon His name.

Augustus Montague Toplady (1740-78)

TODAY'S RESOLVE
Today I will deliberately try to help to solve somebody's problem, big or small, and make God's world a happier place.

PRAYER
Dear Lord, I cannot always understand your actions but I never doubt your love. Show me who needs my help today. Amen,

21: "GOD AND BABYLON"

Reading: Habakkuk 1: 6-11   **(Key: Verse 6)**

"I am sending the Babylonians. They are fierce and cruel-marching across the land, conquering cities and towns."

No, I'm sorry. I can't accept this! I cannot believe that God sends a horde of drunken, murdering, raping, looting mercenaries to punish his disobedient people. Perhaps even Habakkuk himself can't believe it (1:12-17).

I cannot believe it simply because I look at God 'from the other side of Jesus' and know that Jesus would never do such a thing. So Habakkuk has presented me with yet another spiritual conundrum. I cannot accept this scenario, so there is no point in my trying to justify it. However, behind it, lies a significant idea! Can God use ungodly happenings to do his will? There is some mileage in exploring that.

Yesterday, I struggled with the mysteries of God's actions, but I never doubt that God's purposes will be fulfilled – otherwise God stops being God! Surely God can use any part of his creation to achieve a positive outcome but can that really include ungodly things?

The problem of Evil has tormented great minds for centuries and I can't solve it but I realise that there is something that helps me at a practical level.

I have that memory from many years ago, when, in the Shetland Islands, I watched ladies doing 'Shetland knitting' with their leather belts and multiple needles. Working like lightening, they simultaneously drew different coloured wools to their needles. Then, magically, from those needles unfolded a wonderful pattern composed of the darker and the lighter strands.

Perhaps life is like that. Good and bad are woven inextricably together and, in some way that I cannot fully understand, they almost need each other if the garment is to be whole.

God uses that multi-coloured fabric for God's own purposes, and, under Godly hands, even the unholy strands can be put to holy use. I still remember how my very first little Yorkshire chapel was lovingly renovated by its members. How proud we were of our handiwork!

Then, before we could re-open, vandals trashed the vestry and poured paint over everything. We were heart-broken but what a miracle ensued! When the news broke, God touched so many hearts. The local miners, ashamed that 'their chapel' had been desecrated, collected money for us and we were showered with gifts and offers of help from all over the country. It was the 'dark strand' which, in God's hand, became a means of blessing.

The philosophical problem of Evil may be intractable but common human experience testifies that God can use even the worst aspects of life to pour out his blessings. Isn't this the message that streams to me from Calvary and the Cross, so quickly followed by the Resurrection?

Every Good Friday, I try to listen to one of Bach's *Passions* and, as I listen, I relive the inexplicable truth that "God made Him who knew no sin to be sin for us, that we might become the righteousness of God in Him." (*II Corinthians* 5:21) The most evil act in history has become the conduit of the greatest blessing!

It was in the depths of despair that William Cowper wrote a hymn expressing the faith that, one day, he hoped to feel again. I claim it for my own dark days when they come.

Ye fearful saints, fresh courage take.
The clouds ye so much dread
Are big with mercy, and shall break
In blessings on your head.
Judge not the Lord by feeble sense,
But trust Him for His grace;
Behind a frowning providence
He hides a smiling face.

William Cowper (1721-1800)

TODAY'S RESOLVE
I will deliberately find a way to be the instrument of God's blessing to some person or a group of people who are suffering dark times.

PRAYER
Crucified Lord, show me how to be a blessing to someone who is passing through the Valley of the Shadow. Amen

22. "SIX ENGLISH WORDS"

Reading: Habakkuk 2:1-8   **(Key: Verse 4)**

"The just shall live by faith." (KJV)

Only six simple English words but they have torn the Church asunder and changed the history of the world. How dare I call *Habakkuk* a Biblical B-Road when it contains these words!

Nevertheless, I must ignore the theological debates about Justification by Faith. Those are for another time and place. I need to disentangle the original meaning of these words from the later theological debates.

Old Testament experts say that God is warning Habakkuk that, in the dark days to come, only the 'just' or the 'righteous' will survive. These are the people who, although living in the midst of a corrupt nation, have continued to obey God's commandments and have maintained their spiritual discipline.

They 'will survive by their faith' because, their devotional routine has nurtured their faith. They have stored up spiritual food in days of plenty against the forthcoming famine and they will retain their firm confidence in God's promises.

This has set me thinking about the place of 'the discipline of righteousness' in sustaining my own faith.

To be honest, sometimes the routines of faith can seem irksome. Why should I pray when I don't feel like it? Why should I go to church when I'm not in the mood? Why should I read the Bible when it says nothing to me? Why should I give to charity when I need the money for myself? Why bother?

Habakkuk is showing me the value of faithful routine. Each prayer, each act of worship, each Bible study and each charitable gift is another brick built into the wall of 'righteousness'.

Of course, I don't mean that I am saved by my own good works (Paul and Luther can sleep safely!) but that each act of self-discipline helps to create the walls within which my faith-can grow and flourish. Within those walls my trust in God develops and I receive a sort of spiritual blood-transfusion as the power of the Holy Spirit flows into my veins.

That is what Jesus has promised me. He said that, when I have faith in him, he will send the Holy Spirit to empower me, and I realise now that the particular channels of that power are prayer, worship and charity. I need to embrace their discipline 'in season and out of season'.

Come down, O Love Divine,
Seek Thou this soul of mine,
And visit it with Thine own ardour glowing;
O Comforter, draw near,
Within my heart appear,
And kindle it, Thy holy flame bestowing.
O let it freely burn,
Till earthly passions turn

To dust and ashes, in its heat consuming:
And let Thy glorious light
Shine ever on my sight,
And clothe me round, the while my path illuming.

Bianco da Siena d. 1434
Trans. Richard Littledale (1833-90)

TODAY'S RESOLVE
I will examine my regular routine of devotion and see if it needs changing and improving.

PRAYER
Lord, I want to be a disciplined Christian, please show me how to improve my openness to you so that I may receive the gifts you wish to give me. Amen.

23. "THE POWER OF QUIETNESS"

Reading: Habakkuk 2:18-20   (Key: Verse 20)

"Let all the world be still – the Lord is present in his holy temple."

Here are some more words from *Habakkuk* that often appear on Sundays as a Call to Worship. "The Lord is in his holy temple; let the whole earth keep silence before him." What unexpected, familiar riches I am finding along this B-Road!

Habakkuk is reminding me that there are situations when silence is the only proper attitude. I think of the Two Minutes Silence which radiates from the Cenotaph on Remembrance Sunday. No words can express the essence of that maelstrom of national pride, sorrow and resolve.

This is also true in the life of the Spirit. As a student, I can just remember my father preaching a magnificent sermon on the text, "There was silence in heaven for about half an hour". (*Revelation* 8:1) That climactic moment when the Seventh Seal is broken, could only be adequately celebrated by celestial silence.

I don't really think of Woody Allen as a theologian but I do remember his quip, "God is silent! Now, if only man would shut up!"

As I see it, part of our problem is that we live in a society which often regards silence as subversive.

I have just encountered the incredible statistic that the average user spends 3.6 hours a day on their smart phone. Silence seems to be thought of almost as anti-social. Railways have to designate 'Silent Coaches' to muffle passengers' loud, inconsequential telephone conversations. A request to mute noisy music will probably precipitate a Human Rights furore! Let a person be silent in company and it will be assumed that he or she is almost certainly ill, depressed or bad-tempered.

Surely, there is a need for silence when, like Habakkuk, I stand 'in his Temple' and sense the glory and presence of God.

I remember being in Truro Cathedral where the presence of God floats almost palpably in the soaring arches. It should have been a place of such awed silence but, instead, I was beset by groups of loud-gabbling tourists.

However, Habakkuk presents me with a personal challenge. Is the worship that I lead too 'busy'? How lax I have been in helping congregations to cherish the gift of devotional silence! If I announce even a short time of silent prayer during worship, it is quite likely that the first embarrassed cough will erupt after about thirty seconds.

So what am I to make of all this? I think that I have to consider afresh the importance of silence in my Christian life. Sometimes I can't even be quiet when I am saying my own prayers. I just have to keep chattering at God.

Silence does not come naturally to me and it is a discipline that I will have to work at. In my devotions, I need to 'enter the Temple' and there wait until I feel the real presence of God. I have to consider what I do with my silences.

Real mystics can find beatific visions in their silences but for me that may be a step too far. I need to begin at a simpler level and use my silences for listening to God, thinking about the Father, Son and Holy Spirit and understanding God's priorities. Let me see where it leads.

Open, Lord, my inward ear,
And bid my heart rejoice;
Bid my quiet spirit hear
Thy comfortable voice;
Never in the whirlwind found,
Or where earthquakes rock the place,
Still and silent is the sound,
The whisper of Thy grace.

(Charles Wesley 1707-88)

TODAY'S RESOLVE
I will make a start today and find a quiet place where I can take the first steps in developing the discipline of silence.

PRAYER
Lord, I am a terrible chatterer, show me how to be quiet before you and help me to develop Silence in my devotional life. Amen

24: "JOY IN JEOPARDY"

Reading: Habakkuk 3:16-19   (Key: Verses 17-18)

"Though the fig-tree does not bud and there are no grapes...and the fields produce no food, though there are no sheep in the pen and no cattle in the stalls, yet I will rejoice in the Lord, I will be joyful in God my Saviour." (NIV)

I like this translation best. Although he faces so many unsolved difficulties, Habakkuk finishes by writing a performance-song for the Chief Musician and his players. It is a remarkable song.

The prophet writes that, even if the terrible Babylonians come and the nation's whole life-support system collapses, still he will 'be joyful in God his Saviour'.

Now I am very confused. How can he say that God is his 'Saviour' when he obviously *hasn't* saved him'? The merciless Babylonians are still coming and, even if harvests are good and livestock plentiful, they will all be seized by the conquerors and the people will starve.

That doesn't sound much like 'salvation' to me! Yet Habakkuk says that, not only will he accept it, but he will 'rejoice' and 'celebrate'.

Was he some sort of super-believer? Do the great saints 'rejoice' at such times because they are special people who don't feel pressures like I do? I don't think so.

There are few people I admire more than the great German Christian, Dietrich Bonhoeffer who was so calm and brave when he faced his Nazi executioners. However, I can never forget that he once admitted that he was "too tired and empty to pray....and ready to take leave of it all." He felt as I would feel in those circumstances. So what is the secret that sustains the saints?

Habakkuk says that he is 'joyful' because, "The Lord gives me strength... and he helps me stand on the mountains." I think that I understand what he means. It is when he is totally empty and without personal resources that there is most room for the power of God to come in. It is when, like an empty vessel, he has nothing to offer up but his helplessness that he is most completely filled.

I love the idea of God standing the prophet on a mountain. It reminds me of standing on the Malvern Hills and being able to see the counties laid out below me –a vista that I could never have seen when driving around on the plain below.

From his mountain height, Habakkuk can see the true situation. He can be at rest because he can see that God is the supreme ruler of history to whom the fearsome Babylonians are but pawns in a game and bitter events are passing shadows.

I realise that the prophet is teaching me that the only thing that really matters is to put my life, full or empty, rich or poor, easy or difficult, into God's hands and allow God to fill it with whatever power I need.

Thank you, Habakkuk and goodbye.

Leave God to order all thy ways,
And hope in Him whate'er betide:
Thou'lt find Him in the evil days
Thy all-sufficient strength and guide:
Who trusts in God's unchanging love
Builds on the rock that cannot move.
Only thy restless heart keep still,
And wait in cheerful hope, content
To take whate'er His gracious will
His all-discerning love hath sent.

Georg Newark (1621-81)
Trans. by Catherine Winkworth (1829-78)

TODAY'S RESOLVE

I will imagine losing all the things that I hold most precious in my life, although it will hurt. Then I will catch a glimpse of Habakkuk's faith and test my own.

PRAYER

Lord God, stand me on the mountain and give me such a strong faith that I can hold to you in the darkest days. Amen

THE SECOND LETTER OF JOHN

DAY TWENTY-FIVE

25: "THROUGH JESUS' EYES"

Reading: The Second Letter of John   (Key: Verse 2)

"We love you because the truth is now in our hearts and it will be there forever."

Squeezed as they are between the beauties of *John I* and the pyrotechnics of *Revelation*, I have to confess that I have seldom lingered over *John II* and *III*. To my shame, I see that a note in the margin of my Bible shows that I last studied it nearly twenty years ago. It is high time that I walked down this particular Biblical B-Road. The author just identifies himself as 'The Elder' so he must have been well-known to his readers, probably their pastor or bishop. He addresses his letter to 'a very special lady and her children', which may be how he thinks of a particularly beloved congregation.

He says that the two things that have created the special bond within that congregation are 'love' and 'truth' and, immediately, he gives me food for thought. It is good for me to be reminded that a local congregation is a wonderful creation. A Christian congregation is a miracle of divine social engineering, a group of fallible human beings made distinctive by a special bond of love and truth.

Let me begin with 'truth' because I notice that what John talks about is being 'in the truth'. I have heard of 'being in love' but never before of being 'in the truth' and I wonder what John means. I know that 'Truth' is one of his great words and, since Jesus says, "I am the Way, the Truth and the Life' so John must mean that his congregation are 'in Jesus the Truth'. What a wonderful picture this is!

A congregation is made up of people who, like me, want to be so close to Jesus that we are 'in him', surrounded and enveloped by him. Jesus is my Great Truth. He is my clue to understanding everything. He shows me God. He shows me how to live. He gives me the power to follow him and he promises me life beyond death. What more could I want? This is, indeed, a wonderful picture of a congregation but I know that sometimes the reality has seemed rather different. In my time, I have been critical of churches and they have rightly been critical of me. How do we retain that vision of being 'in truth' without being disappointed and frustrated by our mutual imperfections?

An idea has come to me. I remember an old film, *The Singapore Story*, which told how Bishop Wilson was imprisoned by the Japanese in the infamous Changi Prison in eastern Singapore. When asked how he had been able to endure the torture without hating the torturers, he replied that he tried to see his tormentors as they were when they were innocent children. It was by seeing their ideal selves before they became corrupt and cruel that he was able to love them. Surely, it is when I try to see my imperfect fellow Christians as Jesus wants them to be (and hope that they are gracious enough to see me that way too) that the wonderful truth and love of which John speaks will flourish between us. Truth and Love will entwine together and grow gloriously.

'Love' is the other bond in a congregation but 'love' is such an elastic word, it can mean anything from noble dedication to bestial lust. But the love of which John speaks is very special. It is God's love made human in Jesus. John is telling me that, as I live in Jesus so his divine love will flow into me and out from me. As John says, that is love which does not ebb and flow with feelings or fade away with lack of enthusiasm. How I long for that love as a permanent possession! A final thought! I treasure the Communion Hymn in which that old Oxford professor William Bright asks God to see us as he intends us to be.

Look, Father, look on His anointed face
And only look on us as found in Him;
Look not on our misusing of Thy grace,
Our prayer so languid and our faith so dim;
For lo! Between our sins and their reward,
We set the passion of Thy Son our Lord

William Bright (1824-1901)

Now *there's* something for me to ponder!

TODAY'S RESOLVE

Today, I will try and see everybody I meet through the eyes of Jesus and see them as he wants them to be.

PRAYER

Patient and loving Lord, I am so quick to criticise others, please help me to see them as you see them as loved regardless of all their imperfections – and please see me that way too. Amen

26: "MY LOAF WARD"

Reading: The Second letter of John   (Key: Verse 6)

"And this is love, that we walk in obedience to His commandments.   As you have heard from the beginning, His command is that you walk in love." (NIV)

I prefer this translation which seems to me to reflect the original text so well. Having said how important 'love' is, John now defines it and his definition intrigues me. I always think of love as an emotion. Anybody who has ever been 'in love' knows that! It is an all-consuming passion that fills one's entire life-horizon. Yet John speaks of 'love' as a discipline, as 'obedience'. In loving my fellow Christians, he says, I am simply obeying God.

'Obedience' is not a popular word in a society which regards obeying somebody else as a sort of slavery but, John reminds me that Jesus is my 'Lord' to whom I owe willing obedience. As his 'disciple', I am under his 'discipline'. In trying to understand this text, I have dutifully carried out the required study of *kurios* (*'Lord'*). However, being curious, I decided to look up our English word 'Lord' and I made an intriguing discovery. It comes from the two words 'Loaf Ward' – the 'Bread Keeper'. I suppose the idea was that mediaeval peasants obeyed their lord because he controlled their food supply. I like that idea. Jesus is my 'Loaf Ward', he controls my life and I am not free to do what I like with it.

But John has not finished with me. He says that this 'obedience-love' is not a one-off decision; it a process. He describes it as 'a walk'. For me, a 'walk' is gentle exercise with my dog but John warns me that 'obedience-love' is not 'a stroll in the park'; it is a disciplined walk. I have to realise that continuing to love my fellow Christians can sometimes be difficult.

I happen to be reading the life-story of Bob Martyn, a wonderful old saint whom I knew and for whom I had a particular admiration. (I have no doubt that he is now with his 'Loaf Ward' in glory!) I have just read how, as a faithful Methodist Local Preacher, he walked miles through Cornish snow to lead a service only to arrive at a Chapel bearing the notice "SERVICE CANCELLED". Yes, sometimes being 'obediently loving' can be like that, hard going on the way and disappointing on arrival. Christians are not always lovable nor do they always live up to expectations.

Nevertheless, hard though it can be, John reminds me that I signed up to this 'obedience-love' 'from the beginning'. It was one of the first things that I promised to do when I became a Christian. It is as though John knows that, when the going gets tough, I will want to say, "I didn't know it would be like this" or "I don't need to keep my promise in these circumstances." And, of course, he is right! John compliments his readers on their 'obedience-love' but he also warns them that it is going to be tested afresh. Like them, I need to be warned that there will be times when my 'obedience-love' will be tested to its breaking-point. I am reminded that Robert Schuller of the Crystal Cathedral used to say that it is "When the going gets tough, (that) the tough get going."

One last warming thought! I can remember several occasions when, like John, I too have been very proud of my fellow-Christians. There have been times when the life and unity of a congregation have been sorely tested but their 'obedience-love' has triumphed.

Instead of becoming bitter and vengeful, they have been obedient and allowed God's love to flow through them into the challenging situation. At such times I have felt privileged to be among Christians who have been so faithful to their 'Loaf Lord'!

All hail the power of Jesu's name;
Let angels prostrate fall;
Bring forth the royal diadem
To crown Him Lord of all.
O that with yonder sacred throng
We at His feet may fall,
Join in the everlasting song,
And crown Him Lord of all!

Edward Perronet (1734-99)

TODAY'S RESOLVE
Today I will be obedient and look for an extra way to show my loving care for a fellow-Christian.

PRAYER
Jesus, my beloved 'Loaf Ward', give me an opportunity today to show extra love and care to a fellow-Christian. Amen

27: "THE OVER-FAMILIAR GOSPEL"

Reading: The Second Letter of John (Key: Verse 7)

"These deceitful liars are saying that Jesus Christ did not have a truly human body."

I sometimes have trouble with God; simply for being so *'Godlike'*! God deals in a relaxed way with nano-seconds and light years, germs and galaxies, microbes and multiverses, the infinitesimal and the infinite. God is both too 'big' for me and too 'small' for me. When I try to imagine or understand God my mind simply implodes. Is that a terrible admission for a Christian to make? Anyway, it is true for me and, therefore, were it not for the fact that, in Jesus, God shows me what the Godhead is really like; I might sink into a sort of bewildered agnosticism.

Therefore, I understand why John is so disturbed when teachers appear in his congregation claiming that Jesus was not a real man. I don't think that they are being deliberately mischievous; they are simply stating what appears to them to be a respectable theological doctrine.

They argue that, the material world is totally inferior to the spiritual Therefore, there is no way that God would 'downgrade' the divine being and appear as a material human. So, they say, Jesus only *looked* like a human being. He was a sort human hologram, created to do God's work on earth.

As I read this, that early Christian hymn in *Philippians* 2 is coming into my mind. "Christ Jesus...being in the form of God....came in the form of men." I discover that the word 'form' here means 'having the essential characteristics".

Jesus really *is* God and he really *is* human. Reading this old hymn more carefully, I have just realised that it lists what I can only call Layers of Grace in Christ's sacrifice – loss of divinity, surrender of dignity, birth as a human, acceptance of servant-hood, obedience in life and death on a cross. Let me think about this.

When I stop and peel off those remarkable layers, I begin to feel that I may have become over-familiar with the Gospel and have forgotten the immense cost it embodies. If the God of Galaxies loves me that much, then the statistics of salvation are breath-taking.

It is amazing that God creates every human being unique and I suppose that only a God that 'big' can know them all and love them all. The idea that Jesus underwent all that the hymn recites to assure me of my personal involvement in the Divine Plan blows my mind. And yet I am assured that it is true. John tells me that 'The Father and the Son will be with me"

But that idea of being over-familiar with the Gospel still nags. I can't remember a time when it was not the background of everything I did. Of course, I have had my spiritual ups and downs and even managed to be a fanatical student atheist for a while but it has always been there.

Now I have just seen something else. It is when John's congregation is threatened by the false teachers that they lay hold afresh on the treasures of the true Gospel. Perhaps that is the way God uses heresy. It is when my faith is attacked or criticised that I have to analyse it and feel its thrill once more.

Almighty God, Thy Word is cast
Like seed into the ground;
Now let the sun and rain be given,
And righteous fruits abound.
Let not the universal foe
This holy seed remove,
But give it root in every heart
To bring forth fruits of love.

John Cawood (1775-1852)

TODAY'S RESOLVE
I will write down the basic treasures of my Christian faith so that I avoid simply taking them for granted.

PRAYER
Magnificent God, forgive me that I have allowed your greatest miracle of Grace to become 'ordinary'. Resurrect my sense of wonder. Amen.

READING: THE THIRD LETTER OF JOHN

DAY TWENTY-EIGHT

28: "BLESSED HOSPITALITY"

Reading: The Third Letter of John   (Key: Verse 5)

"Dear friends, you have always been faithful in helping other followers of the Lord, even the ones you didn't know before."

I wish that I could have met Gaius. He sounds a wonderful Christian and it's a pity that nobody can identify him for certain. I like to think that, as tradition has it, he is, indeed, made Bishop of Pergamum because I'm sure that he would be a great leader. John says that Gaius has a particular reputation for hospitality. It seems that Christian travellers, even strangers, arriving unannounced at his door are always received with kindness, fed, sheltered and then sent on their way. He is Gaius, the Hospitable.

What a wonderful title! Hospitality, a solemn duty in the Old Testament, in the New is a loving provision especially for fellow-Christians. Paul tells the Galatians that they "should help people whenever they can especially if they are followers of the Lord." (*Galatians* 6:10) I acknowledge that I owe the fact that I am in the church today largely to 'hospitality'. After Sunday evening service, two maiden ladies opened their flat to a crowd of us rowdy teenagers and plied us with simple refreshments. But I have also been blessed by Christian hospitality on many occasions. I still feel both grateful and guilty when I remember a poor Kenyan family who invited us for a meal in their hut. They insisted upon sitting and watching as we ate one of their precious chickens – caught that morning and cooked especially for us. Hospitality between Christians is such a powerful implement of Grace.

However, there is something else. I see that the Greek for 'hospitality' means 'love of strangers'. In other words, Christian hospitality is not just a matter of having my friends come for a meal or pouring morning coffee for my neighbours. The distinctively **Christian** part only begins when, like Gaius, I begin to do those things for 'strangers'. It makes me remember how, during the war, my parents somehow provided extra Sunday lunches from their wartime rations. There was always an invitation for service men and women who had attended the compulsory Church Parade but, afterwards, had nowhere else to go. Most were strangers and we never saw them again but my parents had touched their lives with Christian grace.

I notice something more. John commends Gaius for providing for travellers who are 'helping to spread the truth'. It is a strange fact that, immediately after the Age of the Apostles, not many famous Christian leaders are identified.

The 'missionaries' were the 'ordinary' Christians of whom John speaks, who journeyed along the hundreds of miles of Roman roads, sharing their faith with fellow-travellers. Gaius is blessed for supporting Christian missionaries. Having been a mission partner myself I know just how much it means to know that Christians at home are praying for you and supporting your work.

This has brought something very practical to mind. I hope that every Christian has a specifically chosen missionary cause to which they give regularly and generously. It is so necessary in a world which desperately needs the Gospel because it has never been more difficult to raise funds for the worldwide missionary work of the Church.

So I carry away two rather simple thoughts today. The first is the need for Christian hospitality at home and the second is the need for generous Christian giving to worldwide missionary work. Goodbye John – and thank you!

In Christ there is no east or west,
In Him no south or north,
But one great fellowship of love
Throughout the whole wide earth
Join hands then brothers of the faith
Whate'er your race may be;
Who serves my Father as a son
Is surely kin to me.

John Oxenham (1852-1941)

TODAY'S RESOLVE
    Today, I will review my missionary giving and make sure that it is properly organized and suitably generous.

PRAYER
    Lord Jesus, who lived for a while among us, show me ways in which I can be hospitable to strangers. Amen.

THE SONG OF SOLOMON

DAY TWENTY-NINE

29: "TREAD CAREFULLY!"

Reading: The Song of Solomon C.1   (Key: Verse 1)

"This is Solomon's most beautiful song."

I've made a strange discovery. Commentaries on *The Song* are not very plentiful and when I found one to help me, it was written by one of my old professors. I can still see him sitting in his book-lined study, smoking his pipe and gently exposing the howlers in my Old Testament essays. But I digress!

I am on a new Bible B Road and what a beautiful path it is, bedecked with flowers and sweet-singing birds. Its title means literally, *The Most Beautiful Song of All.* So why do I still feel a little like a naughty school-boy when I open its few pages? Is it because, it seems wrong to have a book in the Bible which includes 'sexy bits'? Perhaps others feel that way too and that is why, for many, this is virtually an untrodden road.

Obviously, I need to sort myself out! However, I need not feel too guilty because, long before me, the Jewish and Christian Fathers obviously felt the same. The Rabbis apparently forbade men under thirty to read *The Song* and the Fathers decided that such a passionate human love story must be a coded picture of the intimate relationship between God and his beloved people.

Seen in this light, it was greatly admired. Gregory of Nyssa calls it 'the Holy of Holies' and virtually all the Church Fathers join in to explain its deeper meaning. I think that it is best to see the book as a series of love poems and, as I wander through them, perhaps I will find myself drawing on various different interpretations.

It is dawning on me that there is a sense in which the Bible would be incomplete without its own special and specific love story. In this first chapter, the girl dreams of her lover just as countless millions of girls have dreamed ever since. Love is so important for humans that it has inspired more songs and poems than any other theme. There is scarcely a story from which love is entirely excluded and few homes exist where its tokens are not to be found on display.

There can be few readers of *The Song* in whom it does not stir personal and private memories. Certainly, I gladly attest that love has been the greatest experience of my life. So away with any sense of unease!

I know that, today, the whole concept of 'love' is dreadfully confused and mutilated, so reading this idyll can be truly therapeutic. The poems force me to wonder afresh about that strange alchemy which takes place between two human beings, transmuting their relationship into pure gold. How is it that they can have many relationships and meet many attractive people and yet, suddenly, they know that 'this is the one'? How did I know that I was 'in love' and nobody else but this particular person would be my life's partner?

I read somewhere that when a man falls in love, he 'recreates his Eve'. He sees his beloved as the perfect woman. The poem shows that the same is true of this girl who sighs, "My love, you are handsome truly handsome." How precious is this memory! Browning's description of the thrush's repeated song comes to my mind, "This first fine careless rapture." Where else could such pure emotion come from but the One whose very essence is Love? The wonderful thing is that when that halcyon relationship is placed in the hands of the God of Love, it grows and flourishes even after mutual imperfections have made themselves felt. I have to be honest and admit that I have dear Christian friends for whom, often for reasons beyond their control, this dream has not come true and I have felt their pain. Nevertheless, the poems hold up God's ideal in a most beautiful way.

Love divine, all loves excelling,
Joy of heaven to earth come down:
Fix in us Thy humble dwelling,
All Thy faithful mercies crown;
Jesu, Thou art all compassion,
Pure, unbounded love Thou art;
Visit us with Thy salvation,
Enter every trembling heart.

Charles Wesley (1707-88)

TODAY'S RESOLVE

Today I will make a mental list of those whose love is so precious to me and I will be truly thankful.

PRAYER

Loving Lord, thank you for teaching me to love and for giving me the love of other people. Let me never take love for granted. Amen.

30: "A DIFFERENT VISTA"

Reading: The Song of Solomon C.2   (Key: Verse 1)

"I am the rose of Sharon and the lily of the valleys"

I can't miss this. I can still remember the youthful gusto with which I sang the chorus about Jesus.

He's the lily of the valley
He's the bright and morning star
He's the fairest of ten thousand.
Everybody ought to know!

I wasn't sure what it meant and I certainly hadn't a clue whence it came but I thought that the words were beautiful. And here it is in its original setting, so I cannot pass it by.

I must ignore the translator's botanical mix-up over the flowers and move into allegorical mode. I remember that Spurgeon preached one of his majestic sermons on, *The Rose and the Lily* but, for my thinking, I'm going to renew my old friendship with the Church Fathers. They use great ingenuity to compare Jesus to Solomon the Bridegroom and, maybe they will give me new insights.

I can begin with the 'lily' (probably not the flower I would recognize) which means 'whiteness' and is the symbol of Purity. I have discovered that, according to *Leviticus,* the basic idea of 'purity' is 'fit for God's presence'. I must confess that I have not often thought about Jesus as the perfect example of Purity but, now that I have, I understand something very moving about Christ the Pure.

When I began preaching, a wonderful old saint gave me a copy of Matthew Henry's, *Commentary on The Whole Bible* and it became my first treasured Bible guide. Reading today's words, I decided to consult it once again and I am glad that I did. Matthew Henry calls the book, "a bright and powerful ray of heavenly light" and says that this verse teaches us that believers share Christ's beauty. "They are as lilies, for those are made like Christ in whose hearts his love is shed abroad." What a brilliant insight!

I am made 'beautiful' by Christ and able to come into God's presence because Jesus has clothed me with his purity. I am reminded of Jude's closing words, "Now to Him who is able to keep you from stumbling and present you faultless before the presence of his glory with exceeding glory."

Now for the 'Rose of Sharon' – not, of course, a rose as I know it but, since it grew in Sharon's fertile soil, it would certainly be the finest of its kind. For the Fathers, the rose is very special. St. Ambrose says that, originally, roses grew smooth-stemmed in Paradise but they developed thorns after The Fall to remind us of the Paradise we lost through sin. The rose became the symbol of martyrdom, so I must place Christ the Martyr beside Christ the Pure. It reminds me of the price that Christ paid in order to clothe me with his purity so that I might come into God's presence. Sacrifice and Sanctification are joined.

Obviously, sometimes it pays me to travel with half-forgotten friends like the Church Fathers. My former spiritual guides have opened my eyes to truths to which otherwise I would have been blind. Christ is the Pure Martyr.

Jesus, Rose of Sharon, bloom within my heart,
Beauties of Thy truth and holiness impart,
That where I go my life may shed abroad
Fragrance of the knowledge of the love of God.
Jesus, Rose of Sharon, sweeter far to see
Than the fairest flowers of earth could ever be
Fill my life completely, adding more each day
Of Thy grace divine and purity, I pray.

Ida A. Guirey (1922)

TODAY'S RESOLVE
Today I will think carefully about Purity and my unworthiness to stand before God

PRAYER
Magnificent and holy God, I thank you that you sent Jesus the Martyr to enable me to come into your presence covered by his Purity given to me at such great cost. Amen.

31: "THE MYSTIC POWER"

Reading: The Song of Solomon   (Key: Verse C8v7)

"Many waters cannot quench love, nor can the floods drown it"

Isn't it strange! Reading *The Song* in *KJV* I find its poetry so beautiful that I almost don't want to pick out any more Key Verses. It reminds me of English lessons at school when we had to dissect great poems for rhythm, rhymes and references. Great poetry destroyed by diagnosis! I am determined not to repeat the mistake with *The Song* but I noticed some interesting items *en route*.

Firstly, I found another line of yesterday's chorus - "He's the fairest of ten thousand" (5:10).

Secondly, I am sure that I had sung a version of 6:10 and finally I have found it. George Wade Robinson's great hymn *Loved with an Everlasting Love* has the refrain, "I am my Lord's and He is mine!"

However, when I come to 8:7 my resolution to travel on fails and I have to stop. A long time ago I wrote a book entitled, *Many Waters Cannot Quench* so how can I pass it by?

As the Bride sings of the incredible power of love, it brings to my mind a thought-provoking coincidence. On a news-stand I saw dozens of 'celebrity' magazines, 'celebrating' the way in which 'celebrities' fall in and out of 'love' as often as they fall in and out of each other's beds. What a sickening counterfeit love!

Then, nearby, a newspaper showed a stumbling Syrian refugee mother who had walked hundreds of miles and braved drowning in treacherous seas just to save her three little children. Now that is Love with a capital 'L'! Quite literally, 'Many waters had not quenched her love'.

I have not done any great things in my life but, looking back, I realise that anything I have achieved has been motivated by love in some form or other. What is this strange power that is found in me and every other human being? Even the 'worst' people are touched by it. How else could Auschwitz guards herd Jewish children into gas chambers during the day and then return home in the evening to play tenderly with their own sons and daughters? Does 'love' well up from fallen human nature or is it an invasive power that overcomes my instincts of self-preservation and self-satisfaction?

It seems to me that it is an invasive power and that its source is the God of Creation. If, as I believe, God is Love, human love is nothing less than an invasion of Divinity. When I truly love, I am given just a little of God's Calvary Love. Perhaps only for a moment, I feel what Jesus felt for me when he allowed the nails to be driven into his hands. How sad it is that so many people do not realise the source of love! How much more they would cherish it if they did! But I know and, the popular phrase truly applies – it is 'awesome'!

Perhaps, after all, dear old Matthew Henry was right. In *The Song*, truly, "there are shallows in which a lamb may wade and depths in which an elephant may swim."

O for a heart to praise my God,
A heart from sin set free;
A heart that always feels thy blood.
So freely spilt for me.
Thy nature, gracious Lord, impart,
Come quickly from above,
Write Thy new name upon my heart,
Thy new, best name of love.

Charles Wesley (1707-88)

TODAY'S RESOLVE
I will deliberately remember those occasions when I have been invaded by God's love and have been able to do something really good.

PRAYER
Loving Lord, thank you for sharing your love with me! Help me to be open to it all the time. Amen.

THE SECOND LETTER OF PETER

DAY THIRTY-TWO

32: "A SPIRITUAL CHECK-LIST"

Reading: II Peter C1:1-9   **(Key:Verses 5-6)**

"Do your best to improve your faith...by adding goodness, understanding, self-control, patience, devotion to God, concern for others and love."

It is little wonder that *the Second letter of Peter* is a Bible B Road! For over three hundred years few Church leaders bothered to use it or even thought that Peter wrote it. Even now, nobody knows for sure when or to whom it was written. Compared with *I Peter*, its language is rough and ready and it is probably the latest book to be included in the New Testament. So ought I to expect very much as I travel through it? Well, I must come to it with an open mind.

The Key verses are promising - an impressive thought from somebody who is supposed to be a 'theological nobody'! I think that this anonymous author (I'll call him 'Peter' and give him some dignity) is going to throw me some challenging ideas. The first one is already here.

I am being told that I must not be content with my basic Christian faith. I must 'add' to it and 'improve' as a Christian. I should be a better Christian this week than I was last! That challenges me because, progress-wise, I think that my Christian life is more gyratory than linear. Each day is very much like its predecessor instead of being "a day's march nearer home". Peter warns me that, if this is to change, it is going to need continual effort on my part and, to help me he gives me a sevenfold check.

The trouble is that every item on Peter's list deserves an essay on its own and there just isn't enough time or space to do them justice. I will just have to slow down and read Peter's words carefully. At first sight it looks to be just a jumble of virtues but, when I think about it, it seems to make really good sense.

Peter says that I must keep in mind that my aim is to be 'good' which he defines as 'being like Jesus'. (1:3) I think that he means that I ought to aim at responding to every situation as Jesus would. That will not come automatically to me so Peter is right to remind me that I need to grow in 'knowledge'. I remember seeing young Christians wearing those WWJD wristbands. Like them in every situation I need to ask, "What would Jesus do" and build up my 'knowledge' of his nature and power.

It seems that Peter knows me very well because he says that I need to develop two virtues- 'self-control' and 'patience'. The New Testament may not talk much about 'self-control' (although Paul says that it is a fruit of the Spirit *Galatians* 5:23) but Peter wisely includes it here. If I am going to be 'good', I need to be 'self-controlled' so that I don't get swept away by difficult circumstances.

What is more, I need to maintain 'self-control' all the time and for that I need 'patience' I like the translation 'perseverance' rather than 'patience' because Peter is telling me that I need 'stickability'. I need to keep on being 'good' even when it becomes very hard.

This means, says Peter, that I need 'devotion to God' which means feeling God's presence and seeing Him at work in every aspect of my life. God is never 'off duty' and neither must I be. I am going to need all the help I can get so finally, says Peter, I must take care to cherish the fellowship of other believers to whom I am bound by *philadelphia* (brotherly love) and *agape* (Christ-like love). What a valuable check-list! 'Peter' is worth listening to. I'll have to go over it again and take my time.

Come, Saviour Jesus, from above!
Assist me with Thy heavenly grace;
Empty my heart of earthly love,
And for Thyself prepare the place.
Nothing on earth do I desire
But Thy pure love within my breast;
This, only this, will I require,
And freely give up all the rest.
Antoinette Bourignon (1616-80)
Trans. by John Wesley

TODAY'S RESOLVE
I will begin today by looking again at Peter's check-list to see what I need to watch carefully during the day. At the end of the day I will look at the check-list again and see how 'good' I have been.

PRAYER
Holy Spirit, help me to be 'good' like Jesus today. Amen

33:"JUST CAMPING OUT"

Reading: II Peter 1:10-21   **(Key: Verses 13-14)**

"I should keep on reminding you until I leave this body, and our Lord Jesus Christ has already told me that i will soon leave it behind."

I have chosen this text because I recently sat by the bed of a dying Christian who, in a lucid moment, told us, as Peter does, "You know that I am dying." Here Peter is challenging me again. What a mystery death is! What thoughts were going through my friend's mind which he could not communicate to us? Was he remembering past events of his life? He said that he was 'ready to go', so did he have a vision of heaven? Was the next world more real to him than the world he was leaving?

I will not know the answers to those questions until I too am being 'called home'. I find myself using that old-fashioned expression 'called home' because it suits Peter's mood. He says that he is leaving 'the tent of this body', in other words he is just 'camping out' in this world until it is time for him to 'go home'. I am puzzled. Why is it that I, like many Christians, do not speak easily about death? Is it that we don't want to? I don't think so. I remember that I preached a sermon on death and expected a fierce negative backlash but the opposite happened. I received many words of appreciation for 'giving permission' for Christians to speak openly about death.

Then, is it because I am caught up in the 'death-denying society's' conspiracy of silence which regards death as a taboo subject? To quote Woody Allen again, "I'm not afraid of death, I just don't want to be there when it happens!"

I am told that many medical professionals are unwilling to speak of death because it challenges their medical omnicompetence. Many 'ordinary' people are silent because they do not know what to say. They no longer have the 'religious mechanism' to deal with it. Thank God that the hospice movement is changing attitudes but still far too many believers are denied 'a good death' –at home surrounded by the family and with dying words of testimony on the lips.

However, I think that there is a more intangible reason for our silence. It is what I call the 'touch wood syndrome'. Deep inside me is the primitive instinct which I saw at work in African curses. It is a sort of 'sympathetic magic', which says that, if I talk about something, I will make it happen. So I see even seasoned Christians who inadvertently mention something unpleasant, immediately 'touch wood' (originally the wood of the Cross) to prevent the worst happening). Do they realise what they are doing?

Peter is reminding me that, no matter what the causes for my reticence, as a Christian I have a responsibility to talk openly about death and correct the cowardly evasions of the world.

Firstly, I declare that death is natural. I am given that godly realism. I am 'only camping' in this world and, when the time is ripe, I will 'go home'.

Secondly, I understand that death is a spiritual matter. I declare that physical death is the prelude to a new spiritual life.

Thirdly, (and I like the way that Peter stresses this) I declare that death is Christocentric. I can't think of a neater word to express the fact that my death is dominated by Jesus. He has been my companion in this life and he will not abandon me in my life-to-come. I have all sorts of unanswered questions about death but my really important questions have been answered in Jesus.

Thank you again 'Peter'.

Happy the souls to Jesus joined,
And saved by grace alone;
Walking in all the ways, we find
Our heaven on earth begun.
The church triumphant in Thy love,
Their mighty joys we know;
They sing the Lamb in hymns above,
And we in hymns below.

Charles Wesley (1707-88)

TODAY'S RESOLVE

Today, as a Christian, I will calmly consider my death, confronting my anxieties and celebrating my certainties. I will no longer be part of the conspiracy of silence.

PRAYER

Loving Lord, you brought me safely into this life and I trust you to bring me safely into the life to come. Calm my fears and strengthen my certainties in Jesus. Amen.

34: "BALAAM'S DONKEY"

Reading: II Peter 2:`1-16   (Key: Verses: 15-16)

"They have left the true road and have gone down the wrong path by following the example of the prophet Balaam corrected by a donkey."

This furious tirade against false teachers is almost a re-run of *Jude* and even Balaam gets a mention in both (*Jude* v.11). However, side-stepping this tricky textual problem, I have to declare my love for donkeys and my fury whenever I saw them being mistreated in Africa. So hard-working and patient, they deserve their thirty biblical references. But of all the 'donkey' stories (apart from Palm Sunday) I like best, the story of Balaam. (*Numbers* 22)

I remember that it is the story of a prophet whose greed makes him ready to sell his services to the Moabites for whom he agrees to curse Israel. After many warnings, he is finally rebuked by his donkey who, having more spiritual understanding than his master, sees an angel barring their path. I like the word Peter uses here for the donkey's 'human voice' which simply means "to make a loud noise" for even I can't claim that the bray of the donkey is beautiful.

Nevertheless, it has set me thinking. When God's people sell themselves and leave the true path, God uses the most unexpected instruments to call them back. This has revived a feeling that I wish would go away but it won't. It is this. Is God using the social, political and economic pressures in our society to bring the Church to its senses? (I notice that Peter appropriately calls Balaam's fall 'insanity')

Just think of the mistakes we have made. In our denominational rivalry we built far too many churches which, now, we have to close. In our doctrinal squabbles, we vilified those who disagreed with us and so multitudes have cried "a plague on all your houses" and have developed their own 'pick and mix' spirituality. In our spiritual myopia we have developed an incestuous form of worship designed to suit our own devotional tastes. People excluded from our liturgical 'codes' have voted with their feet and left us to worship by ourselves. In our unholy alliance with worldly values we have become so obsessed with property, administration and income that crowds, seeing our betrayal of the One who 'had not where to lay his head', have found other ways doing good in the world.

Now, of course, I know that this is a naive over-simplification of a complex situation but I cannot avoid the feeling that there is an uncomfortably large kernel of truth in it. What is more, I cannot deny my part in the charade. I have helped to create this Church which, in that hideous political jargon, is 'no longer fit for purpose'. I am not blind to the glories of the Church even as it is today but I remember also William Temple's disturbing words, "The Church is the only society to exist for the benefit of non-members." I must hear what God is saying through the 'Balaam's Donkey' of voices and influences outside the Church. I believe that the world is urging us to return to proclaiming the Gospel – even though, perversely, it probably will never thank us for doing so!

This makes me ask, "Why should people give our churches a second chance? Even more, what is the Gospel'? My immediate response (although I am sure that there are many better ones) is that it is the Good News that, through Jesus, God has given us the Holy Spirit's power to change individual lives and societies. That is certainly enough for me now. Thank you, 'Balaam's Donkey'.

I'm not ashamed to own my Lord,
Or to defend His cause,
Maintain the honour of His word.
The glory of His cross.
Jesus, my God, I know His name,
His name is all my trust;
He will not put my soul to shame,
Nor let my hope be lost.

Isaac Watts (1674-1748)

TODAY'S RESOLVE
Today, I will take time to measure my life against that definition of The Gospel and see how this can bless the life of my church.

PRAYER
Dear Lord, forgive me for my part in your Church's straying and show me how I can help in its return to the true path. Amen.

35: "DEATH BY A THOUSAND QUIPS"

Reading: II Peter 3:1-13   **(Key: Verse 3)**

"They will make fun of you and say, 'Didn't your Lord promise to come back?   ... the world hasn't changed a bit."

I have to confess that I'm a bit confused about the Second Coming. It's not that I don't believe that it will happen but I really can't sort out its timetable and mechanics. So I understand how Peter's readers felt when they expected Jesus to come back very quickly and it just didn't happen. I'll just have to take Peter's advice and leave it all in God's hands.

However, the reaction of the believers' critics has caught my eye. "They will make fun of you." Now, of course, I know that Christians have always been mocked and that a few insults are nothing compared with the martyrdom of hundreds of my Christian brothers and sisters, who are being killed for their faith. Nevertheless, I want to pursue this idea.

It has become an issue for me because mockery of my faith now comes with all the sophistication of modern media. Christianity (but significantly seldom Islam) is a standard ingredient of the comedians' trade. If they run out of material, all they have to do is to press the right key on their lap-tops and they can find, 'A Thousand Jesus Jokes' to add to their repertoire. Their intended message for me as a Christian is clear. If only I were not so stupid, I would see that being a Christian is ridiculous. The only reason that I don't laugh at their jokes is because I am a hypocrite with no sense of humour.

The trouble is that this approach is 'catching' and even well-meaning people I meet can patronise me in a most irritating way. They imply that I am a nice person but that it is a pity that I am so inadequate that I need 'a religious prop'. Sometimes it is innocuous enough. There is a special sort of jocularity reserved for clergy. "Say one for me"; "You only work one day a week." "You're alright! You have a direct line to heaven" – and so on. Annoying though it is, it can sometimes open a worthwhile conversation. So how ought I to react when people make fun of my faith?

There is a positive side to all this. I ought to be proud to be in excellent company. They mocked my Lord too and it is a privilege to stand with Jesus. Moreover, I ought to be glad that, at least, they think that my faith is worth mocking. Nobody makes jokes about non-subjects. It would be much worse if they simply ignored my Christianity as totally irrelevant.

On the negative side, I can't simply ignore the attacks. If I do, I'm likely to become a Christian snail, withdrawing into my shell whenever there's a whiff of ridicule. However, I must not collude with attacks and simply pretend to join in the 'fun'. That would be like joining the scoffers at the foot of the Cross, a feeble, opportunist betrayal of my Lord. So what must I do?

My problem is that I *do* have a sense of humour and I am able to laugh at myself. In all honesty,

I find some of the jokes are harmless and funny but where do I draw the line? It is not easy but let caution be my watchword. If I find a joke offensive then I must show it by not joining in the general laughter or by making a tactful protest. I don't have to embark upon a tirade which might render my act of witness ineffective. However, if I say nothing, I simply confirm the belief that not even the followers of Christ now regard their faith as special

Perhaps I am being too sensitive – but that is how I feel.

Then learn to scorn the praise of men,
And learn to lose with God;
For Jesus won the world through shame
And beckons thee His road.
For right is right, since God is God,
And right the day shall win;
To doubt would be disloyalty,
To falter would be sin.

Frederick William Faber (1814-63)

TODAY'S RESOLVE
If somebody insults my Lord today, I will not let it pass without appropriate comment.

PRAYER
Lord, I need the 'Wisdom of Solomon' to know how to protest without making matters worse. Please give me the guidance of the Holy Spirit so that I say the right thing in the right way. Amen.

36: "CLOSING THE BOOK"

Reading: II Peter 3:14-18   **(Key: Verse 18)**

"Let the wonderful kindness and understanding that comes from our Lord and Saviour Jesus Christ help you to keep on growing. Praise Jesus now and forever! Amen.

Such wonderful words to end a seldom-explored book! Before leaving, Peter gives me some excellent advice and I love him for it. First of all, he reminds me that, although I have been a Christian for a long time, I am still imperfect and I must keep on growing.

It was Michael Green who said that, "The Christian life is like riding a bicycle. Unless you keep moving, you fall off" – and that is true. However, since I have already thought about the need to grow, I am going to concentrate on the two things that Peter urges me to ask from Jesus

The first is 'wonderful kindness' or 'grace'. 'Grace' is such a rich word. It is like a spiritual treasure-chest. When I open it, I find that it is crammed full of ideas and meanings. Since 'grace' is something that gives pleasure, beauty and delight; 'gracious people' are those who touch the lives of others with all those blessings.

So often, I have ended meetings with, 'May the grace of our Lord Jesus Christ...' without really remembering what I am saying. In fact, I am asking that the 'wonderful kindness of Jesus' will pervade my life and the lives of my fellow-worshippers.

Now that I have stopped to think about it, I find that it is a disturbing thought. Am I really the kind of person who is so touched by Jesus that my life is beautiful with his beauty? Am I a delight as he is a delight and a joy to all who meet me – as he is 'Joy to the world'? I hardly think so. I do well to ask him to keep on filling me with Grace!

The second gift I must seek is, 'understanding'. A better translation is 'knowledge of our Lord'. In other words, I need always to be asking Jesus to teach me more about Him and the whole spiritual aspect of living. I've come to realise over the years that being a Christian is not primarily a matter of accepting a set of beliefs or a code of conduct.

It is more like falling in love and getting married. It is growing in a deep personal relationship with highs and lows, depths and shallows because it involves a continual growth in understanding of Jesus. It is a process which never stops so it is right for me to ask Jesus to continue to help me. If I stop growing in 'understanding', I atrophy and die.

I find the closing words very moving. Peter is writing to a church with big problems but he ends by urging them to "Praise Jesus now and forever. Amen". It reminds me of the words my Kenyan students would say when they were facing some new problem – imminent exams, lack of fees, domestic crises in their homes far away. They would simply say, "Praise Jesus anyway!"

If Peter has taught me nothing else but the need to say, "Praise Jesus Anyway" – walking along his B Road has been well worthwhile.

The world and Satan's malice
Thou, Jesus, hast confounded;
And by Thy grace
With songs of praise.
Our happy souls resounded.
Accepting our deliverance,
We triumph in Thy favour,
And for the love
Which now we prove
Shall praise Thy name for ever.

Charles Wesley (1707-88)

TODAY'S RESOLVE
If, today, I run into problems, I will say 'Praise Jesus anyway' and move on.

PRAYER
Loving Lord, continue to work on our relationship so that I may become a deeper Christian and give me the ability to praise you whatever happens. Amen.

NAHUM

DAY THIRTY-SEVEN

37: "FAITH'S PRESENT TENSE"

Reading: Nahum Chapter One   (Key: Verse 15)

"Behold on the mountains, the feet of him who brings good tidings, who proclaims peace. O Judah, keep your appointed feasts, perform your vows."(NKJV)

I can't remember the last time I read *Nahum* and, having looked again at commentaries I now know why! Comments like "an exultation over the fall of Nineveh", "of no religious value" and "the work of a false prophet" hardly sound encouraging but I must give it a try. It can't be all bad!

I understand why Nahum is so bitter about his vicious Assyrian conquerors but, for all its faults, his little book is an exceptional piece of Hebrew poetry which says important things about God's patience and justice.

However, try as I may, nothing 'sparks' for me until I come to 1:15. There it is - an oasis in the desert! As I read it, memories come flooding back of soaring sopranos singing *How Beautiful are the Feet* from Handel's *Messiah.* That is how most people know these words but they are always attributed to Isaiah (52:7) even though Nahum's version possibly came first.

116

Anyway, I'm going to give Nahum the credit and what lovely, encouraging words they are. He says to the people, "Get on with your lives and worship normally because Assyria has been defeated." What makes this special is that the defeat probably had not yet happened but still Nahum writes in the present tense.

He is so confident in God that he regards the good news as an accomplished fact! I find that a rebuke. Am I so confident that God keeps his promises that I treat them as already fulfilled and just get on with my life? I don't think so. Nahum's name means 'Comforter' but he certainly hasn't comforted me!

It reminds me of that old sermon illustration about a great saint (the name varies with the preacher's source-book) who, faced by a problem, paces the floor of his study into the early hours. Finally, he hears a divine voice saying, "............. go to bed and let me go on worrying instead". Whoever the saint was, it's a great story. Oh, if only I had such confidence in God that I would just, 'go to bed and let Him do the worrying'!

As a Christian I should obey the word of my Lord who urges me to be realistic about my problems. Jesus says, "Can worry make you live longer?" (*Matthew* 6:27).

In fact, worrying makes matters worse but it isn't easy to stop thinking about my problems. I suppose that is why Jesus tells me deliberately to crowd out negativity with everyday examples of God's faithfulness - flowers, birds and the wonders of nature.

I want Nahum's confidence always to write God's promised help in the present tense and then relax. I don't have that confidence yet but I can pray for it next time I face a problem.

Give to the winds thy fears,
Hope and be undismayed:
God hears thy sighs and counts thy tears,
God shall lift up thy head.
Leave to His sovereign sway
To choose and to command;
So shalt thou wondering own His way
How wise and strong His hand.
Paul Gerhardt (1607-76)
Trans. by John Wesley

TODAY'S RESOLVE

Today, I will bravely look at any problems I have and be honest about the things over which have no control, no matter how much I am tempted to worry.

PRAYER

Compassionate Lord, I am not good at not worrying. Help me to be realistic about my problems and to trust you completely. Amen

DAY THIRTY-EIGHT

38: "THE BRIGHT SUCCESSION"

Readings: Matt 1:1-17, Luke 3:23-28   Genealogies!

I might think that, with the contemporary enthusiasm for tracing one's ancestors, the Gospel genealogies would be favourite reading among Christians but they are not. I have to acknowledge that, until quite recently, I have tended to skip over them but now my curiosity has been aroused. I have always known that the genealogy of Jesus was very important for the first Christians. It was necessary to substantiate their claim that he was truly Jewish and that he was the long-expected Messiah.

However, when I finally began to compare Matthew's version with Luke's all kinds of interesting facts emerged – too many to think about now. I have had fun spotting the names I recognize and looking up the Bible references to see what they did. It has made me wonder why I have not done it before.

There is one particular thing that puzzles me. I have always thought of Luke as being the 'women's champion' among the Gospel writers and, indeed, some scholars claim that he gives us Mary's genealogy. However, it is Matthew who mentions five women in the lineage of Jesus. What is more, they are not all saintly. There is a seductress (Tamar), a prostitute (Rahab) and an adulteress (Bathsheba) Nevertheless, Matthew acknowledges the place of women in Jesus' family tree and that sets me thinking about the importance of women in my own family tree – my grandmothers, my mother, my wife and my daughters and, from that, my mind moved on to think about the part that women have played in my own spiritual pilgrimage.

Of course, I remember my mother who said prayers with me when I was very young and taught me what it means to be a committed Christian. But there were remarkable ladies outside my family circle.

I think of my first Sunday School Superintendent in George Street Methodist Church in Worcester- a lovely lady who, faithfully every Sunday told me the stories of Jesus. I think of those ladies in Leyton Tabernacle who opened their flat to us teenagers and lubricated my faith with tea and sympathy.

I think of Mrs. Bennett in my very first church in a Yorkshire mining village; a feisty little lady, who always wore a hat, especially when leading the Monday Women's Bright Hour. She was so much at ease with her Lord that she chatted to him in her prayers and asked for favourable conditions for 'washing day'.

I think of the wonderful succession of lady Church Stewards who have guided my ministry, gently chiding me when I was being foolish and mothering me when I was downhearted. They are all part of my spiritual genealogy and I am thankful for every one of them.

I understand why my Roman Catholic friends venerate the Virgin Mary and, in my own careful Protestant way, I honour her above all other women. She is the Supreme Lady in my spiritual genealogy because, without her humble obedience I would have no Lord to follow. Two of the loveliest lines that Philip Doddridge ever wrote appear in his hymn for Ascensiontide. Writing of all who carry on their Master's work, he says-

So shall the bright succession run,
Through the last courses of the sun.

My spiritual genealogy certainly reveals 'a bright succession' of godly women to whom I am eternally indebted. I don't think that I have finished yet with my study of the Gospel genealogies.

The Saviour, when to heaven He rose,
In splendid triumph or His foes,
Scattered His gifts on us below,
And wide His royal bounties flow.
So shall the bright succession run
Through the last courses of the sun;
While unborn churches by their care
Shall rise and flourish large and fair,

Philip Doddridge (1702-51)

TODAY'S TASK

I will take time to visualise the women who have helped my spiritual growth and thank God for them.

PRAYER

Lord Jesus, son of Mary, I thank you for all the women who have guided my life as she once guided yours. The work still continues, so help me to be sensitive to it and grateful for it. Amen

HAGGAI

39: "FIRST THINGS FIRST"

Reading: The Prophecy of Haggai C1 (Key: Verse 9)

"You hurry off to build your own houses, while My temple still stands in ruins."

I like Haggai but I find him uncomfortable because he reminds me of the importance of getting priorities right in my life. He is writing at a time when God's people returning from exile have lost their original vision and enthusiasm. The crops have failed and the poor people are starving.

So, Haggai addresses the nation's wealthy leaders who have 'feathered their own nests'. His message is clear. Everything has gone wrong because you have put your own comfort first. You have built 'rich houses' for yourselves while God's temple still lies in ruins. Honour God as your priority and all will be well. Of course, Haggai does not mean that the people will have no problems but he insists that, once God is at the centre, they will be able to face them and deal with them.

I am uncomfortably amused by the way that the rich people reply, "Of course, you are right. We must build the Temple but not **now**, the time is not ripe." That's me all over! I know what I ought to do but I can think of a dozen reasons why I should not to do it **now**. But that will not let me off the hook.

My Lord tells me to 'seek first the Kingdom of God' and everything else will follow. In practice that means giving priority to God's will for me without deviation or delay.

Looking back, I can see that God has had major priorities for my life and Haggai is right. When I have not given God priority, things have tended to fall apart. However, I have just been given another idea.

God has 'little' priorities for me too. Reading the biography of St. Francis de Sales –a favourite saint of mine, I see that, in his daily prayer book, he wrote what he called *Preparation*. That meant that the first thing he would see each morning was a list of the duties and responsibilities that awaited him. It was his way of establishing the divine priorities for that day. That is important too. God's priorities for me are not only wide-sweeping and general but also daily and particular. When I discover them and accept them, the day will be properly 'balanced' if I do not it will be out of kilter.

One last thought. God's priorities for my day may not also be mine and I must be ready to change. I think of that occasion when I had my day correctly planned but, during my Quiet Time, the name of a friend was forced into my mind. I could see no reason for this but I felt that I must contact him. I did and, unknown to me, he was in great need. Coincidence or God's new priority?

O Jesus Christ, grow Thou in me,
And all things else recede;

My heart be daily nearer thee,
From sin be daily freed.
Make this poor self grow less and less,
Be Thou my life and aim;
O make me daily, through Thy grace,
More meet to bear Thy name.
Johann Caspar Lavater (1741-1801)
Trans. Elizabeth Lee Smith

TODAY'S RESOLVE
Today, I will take a minute or two to discover God's priorities for me and I will arrange to deal with them.

PRAYER
Lord, thank you for taking an interest in my life and for having a plan for me. Help me to understand it and follow it. Amen.

40: "JOY AMONG THE RUINS"

Reading: The Prophecy of Haggai C2 (Key: Verse 9)

"I promise that this new temple will be more glorious than the first one."

Haggai says that the older people who can remember the former temple must be heart-broken to see it now – just a ruined heap. Surely there can be no prophetic word more touching for today.

I often have just the same feeling about the Church. I remember its glory and confidence in the years when I was growing up and beginning my ministry. Even allowing for nostalgia's ability to remove wrinkles and to double the true size of congregations, it was still glorious. Now, sometimes, the Church I knew seems to be a ruined remnant of its former self. Yes, I can understand the heart-break of those people.

But can I believe God's promise that the coming Church will be 'more glorious than the former'? I would be a liar if I said that I find that easy. With the eye of worldly realism, I see declining attendances, falling membership and closing churches. To deny that would be stupid and dishonest. Yet I know that that is but a small part of the story. The Church in Europe may seem to be numerically in decline but elsewhere the Church is growing and vigorous.

I have seen the congregations queuing outside already overcrowded churches. I have laughed with delight at the singing, clapping and dancing of vibrant congregations. I have seen new churches built and old churches enlarged.

I have seen all that and know that there is still glory in the Church.

However, I am there no longer. Like Haggai's readers, I feel that I am here sitting in the ruins of my memories. So what am I to do? I must either, dissolve in despair and admit that my Lord died on Calvary to leave his church as a picturesque ruin or I must heed Haggai's message. He tells me that ruins only remain ruins if they are neglected.

I might wish that I was living in another time and place but God has put me here for this time and this place because he needs workers to help to rebuild the ruins. In every age, he has continued to work through his 'righteous remnants' and today is no exception.

I can rejoice because I see wonderful new churches springing up and they seem 'more glorious' than those they replace but I believe that God is also at work among those churches which, though smaller in numbers, are still rich` in spirituality. There is spiritual depth, enthusiasm and dedication to be found in many of today's smaller churches.

There is little *kudos* to be gained today by being a Christian – probably the very reverse. Perhaps, in a strange way churches have been 'purified' by the loss of 'hangers on' who once found social acceptance by church-going. Nevertheless, churches must never become spiritually proud, complacent 'holy huddles'. Their purpose is evangelistic not exclusivist.

So it is a privilege to help to revitalize such churches. The work will be as hard as was the restoration of the Temple ruins and I will need to hear again God's word to Haggai, 'cheer up' and 'be strong' because the 'Spirit is right here with me." I cannot predict the form of the revived churches but I do know that, if they are faithful, God will replace their outdated form, with something gloriously new. Hallelujah!

Come, ye that love the Lord,
And let your joys be known;
Join in a song with sweet accord,
While ye surround His throne:
Let those refuse to sing
Who never knew our God;
But servants of the heavenly King
May speak their joys abroad.

Isaac Watts (1674-1748)

TODAY'S RESOLVE
Today is will do everything that I can to work in my church with enthusiasm and to help to spread an atmosphere of confidence in God.

PRAYER
Lord, your people have always faced hard times and it is happening again. Help me to discern your way ahead for my church and to work towards it with bravery and confidence. Amen.

AN EPILOGUE

Thank you for walking with me and taking the time to look over my shoulder. I will miss your company. I hope that some of my insights may have inspired you to have fruitful spin-off ideas of your own. Hopefully, you will stray more regularly into neglected books of the Bible and will invite others to walk with you.

My thanks go to Steve Wild for his encouraging, if over-generous, Foreword. Steve, a former student of mine, is now an eminent Methodist minister whose genius for evangelism is legendary. His words are greatly valued,

As ever, I am grateful to my friend Richard for editing the text, correcting the grammatical howlers and expunging the typographical errors. It is also to him that I owe the insightful advice to enrich our Lenten journey with verses from appropriate hymns. I have chosen these from 'classic' hymns with the traditional words because, in the midst of the glorious cascade of contemporary hymns and worship songs, we must never forget the treasures of the past.

Finally, and to stay in tune with the underlying theme of this Lenten journey that we have shared together, we will allow Jude to have the last word in our personal preparation for the Easter Celebration.

Now, to Him who is able to keep you from stumbling and to present you faultless before the presence of His glory with exceeding joy, to God our Saviour who alone is wise, be glory and majesty, dominion and power, both now and forever. Amen.

Lightning Source UK Ltd.
Milton Keynes UK
UKOW02f0410131216
289854UK00001B/36/P